MACRAMÉ

A Step-by-Step Guide with 29 Projects to Create Stunning Plant Hanger Backdrops and Wall Art

CATERINE RANAE

Copyright - 2021 -

All rights reserved.

The content contained within this book may not be reproduced, duplicated or transmitted without direct written permission from the author or the publisher.

Under no circumstances will any blame or legal responsibility be held against the publisher, or author, for any damages, reparation, or monetary loss due to the information contained within this book. Either directly or indirectly.

Legal Notice:

This book is copyright protected. This book is only for personal use. You cannot amend, distribute, sell, use, quote or paraphrase any part, or the content within this book, without the consent of the author or publisher.

Disclaimer Notice:

Please note the information contained within this document is for educational and entertainment purposes only. All effort has been executed to present accurate, up to date, and reliable, complete information. No warranties of any kind are declared or implied. Readers acknowledge that the author is not engaging in the rendering of legal, financial, medical or professional advice. The content within this book has been derived from various sources. Please consult a licensed professional before attempting any techniques outlined in this book.

By reading this document, the reader agrees that under no circumstances is the author responsible for any losses, direct or indirect, which are incurred as a result of the use of information contained within this document, including, but not limited to, - errors, omissions, or inaccuracies.

TABLE OF CONTENTS

INTRODUCTION — 7
    WHY IS SOMETHING MACRAMÉ? — 9
    MACRAMÉ DESKTOP — 10
    THE BACKGROUND OF MACRAMÉ — 10
    MACRAMÉ MATERIALS — 13

CHAPTER - 1
    TOOLS AND MATERIALS — 13
    GENERAL SUPPLIES — 14
    TOOLS — 15
    GLUE — 17
    PINS — 17
    CORDS AND BEADS — 18
    CORD MEASUREMENT — 20
    CHINESE CROWN KNOT — 23

CHAPTER - 2
    KNOTS AND TECHNIQUES — 23
    SQUARE KNOT — 24
    ALTERNATING SQUARE KNOTS — 25
    LARK'S HEAD KNOT — 27
    REVERSE LARK'S HEAD KNOT — 28

	PROJECT 1: MACRAMÉ FRINGE TASSEL PILLOW:	31
CHAPTER - 3		
	MACRAMÉ PILLOWS, DREAM CATCHER PLUS WRAPPING TECHNIQUES	31
	PROJECT 2: GIFT WRAP	33
	PROJECT 4: MACRAMÉ BRACELET WITH RATTAIL CORD AND GLASS BEADS	47
CHAPTER - 4		
	MACRAMÉ BRACELETS I	47
	PROJECT 5: BLACK AND RED MACRAMÉ BRACELET	53
	PROJECT 6: FISH BONE MACRAMÉ BRACELET	57
	PROJECT 7: SIDE BY SIDE MACRAMÉ BRACELET	61
	PROJECT 8: CROSS CHOKER	67
CHAPTER - 5		
	MACRAMÉ BRACELETS II	67
	PROJECT 9: MACRAMÉ BEADED WAVE BRACELETS	72
	PROJECT 10: RAINBOW BOWS MACRAMÉ BRACELET	77
	PROJECT 11: BEADED HALF MACRAMÉ BRACELET	82
	PROJECT 12: SERENITY BRACELET	87

CHAPTER - 6
   MACRAMÉ BRACELETS III   87

   PROJECT 13: LANTERN BRACELET   93

   PROJECT 14: CELTIC CHOKER   98

   PROJECT 15: CLIMBING VINE KEYCHAIN   103

CHAPTER - 7
   MACRAMÉ BRACELET IV   103

   PROJECT 17: STRIPED CLUTCH
   HANDBAGS   117

CHAPTER - 8
   MACRAMÉ PATTERN: FASHION ITEM   117

   PROJECT 18: PLANT HANGER AYLA   129

CHAPTER - 9
   PLANT HANGERS   129

   PROJECT 19: PLANT HANGER BELLA   133

   PROJECT 20: PLANT HANGER CATHY   138

   PROJECT 21: MODERN MACRAMÉ
   HANGING PLANTER   143

CHAPTER - 10
   **BACKDROP, WALL ARTS,
   HOME DECORS**   143

   PROJECT 22: MINI MACRAMÉ PLANTERS 146

   PROJECT 23: AMAZING MACRAMÉ
   CURTAIN   147

   PROJECT 24: MACRAMÉ WALL ART   149

PROJECT 25: HANGING MACRAMÉ VASE 153

PROJECT 26: EASY DIY MACRAMÉ
PLANT HOLDER   161

CHAPTER - 11
OTHER THINGS YOU CAN DO
IN MACRAME   161

PROJECT 27: MACRAMÉ PLANT HOLDER 162

PROJECT 28: EASY DIY MACRAMÉ
WALL HANGING   163

PROJECT 29: MAKE A HANGER FOR
YOUR WOODEN DOWEL   165

CONCLUSION   173

INTRODUCTION

Macramé is a type of textile manufacturing that does not require the conventional method of weaving or knitting, but alternatively by means of a set of knots. It is considered to have started since the 13th century in the western hemisphere with all the Arab weavers. Any ribbons or threads left over from the ends of both hand-woven cloths, such as towels, veils and shawls, shall not be turned into decorative fringes. What we found fascinating is that the sailors had been people who genuinely created this appeal and have been blamed for dispersing this art to various states through the vents it would stop. They decorated the handles of knives, bottles and other things that could possibly be discovered on the boat and used them to find something they wanted or desired when they came ashore. In reference to this, 19th century sailors generated hammocks and straps with an activity called "square foot".

The materials often used for macramé are cotton yarn,

hemp, thread or leather. Although there are variations, the main knots would be the square knot, although the full feasibility and double half hitch. Jewelry is usually developed by mixing ribbons with diamonds, rings or cubes. In case you look at the vast majority of friendship bracelets worn out by college kids, you will learn that they have been created with Macramé.

After I had been analyzing up about this basic knots, which are often utilized in creating Macramé, I came round the cavaedia Macramé. This design comprises two colors that will be consists of 2 main knots which can be left making a milder sort of fabric which works great for dining table mats, purses, and publication etc. Along with covers, Cavaedia Macramé is well known as Valentina cavaedia who gained a golden trophy of fame out of 1961 before she passed on at age 97 in 1969. Back in Italy through the entire conclusion of this first world war that this exceptional lady became the headmistress of a house in to the evil or orphaned kids in turn. This really is a center where approximately 100 youths may possibly be placed between the ages of 1-5. To keep the children busy, she educated them in an art she had heard from her great-grandmother, Macramé. Records were created of children entering the orphanage, and the grandmother of their marital savings gave a portion to each child when they left the house. Unfortunately, his house, in which he lived until 1936, due to the political situation in Italy as it was difficult to maintain by the benefactors of his house.

The enthusiasm for Macramé appeared to fade

for some time, but was widely used from the 1970's from the American neo-hippies as well as grunge audiences in producing jewelry. This art was comprised in handmade bracelets, anklets and bracelets adorned with handmade glass beads and natural elements such as shell and bone.

Macramé is a fun craft to attempt and you will begin with only a very small budget. You may come across a good deal of cheap or free layouts provided and a few great just how-to novels that will help make you started. This may be an ideal craft to maintain your kids, grandchildren, or anyone busy.

This technique will likely be open to a degree because of its own viability. Unexpectedly, it is very likely to generate things with only the hands using cheap supplies.

Why is Something Macramé?

Macramé is a procedure or procedure of making a fabric that utilizes many knots to produce the very straightforward form and role of this product. Each can possibly be made alongside your palms, and then there are not any tools demanded apart from the routine ring to help keep the merchandise installed since you are working out.

To contemplated Macramé, the Endeavor will have a minimum of one Macramé knot. Ordinarily, Macramé activities are pieced with numerous knots. Occasionally, you have Macramé components combined along with various techniques such as pruning or knitting.

Macramé Desktop

In today's background, Macramé Is still an art type that is attracted west of Arab nations. Weavers from utilizing this component of earth used many knotting ways to complete the great things about things with fringe.

Fabrics were spread through Europe, everyone started to test out knotting for pastime.

Girls were not the only real folks practicing Macramé. Sailors would beg for functional purposes, however on extended voyages, the exercise of knotting functioned like a means to keep engaged. Once they entered new waters, they could swap the Macramé items they left the boat. Popular items contained hats and straps.

A flexible Form of fiber piece, macramé can potentially be employed to make everything from figurines into jewelry, bags, in addition to clothes items. Embellishments such as wooden or glass beads, combined with colored threads, also can open a collection of creative chances.

Know a bit in the intriguing background of the macramé before going with the fundamental methods and tips to find the ideal approach to begin creating your own personal macramé.

The Background of Macramé

Macramé's origins are intriguing. Some think that the expression will come from the term miasma, meaning "fringe". Additional women and men believe its roots lie at the macramé, which explains towel and is still a means to resolve items of pruning using extortionate threads around the underside of woven material.

In almost any event, decorative macramé first seems in followed by Assyrians that portray fringed braiding utilized to decorate drapes. After that, it disperse into Europe throughout North Africa, which brought macramé into Spain.

Such a wonderful way to expend sometime and could be sold to bring into areas such as China and the newest world. Hammocks, straps, together side bell fringes are a range of these favorite by American and British sailors by the 19thcentury. Texts like 1877's the royal macramé lace publication regarding different layouts and knots, reveal just how sexy the procedure had been presently moment.

After taking some fame, macramé found a Resurgence. It finally succeeds and are normally somewhat cyclical. Today, macramé comes directly from artisans who make modern designs with the historic knotting procedures.

CHAPTER - 1
Tools and Materials

Macramé Materials

Macramé stylists make use of different types of materials. The materials can be classified in two major ways: the natural materials and the synthetic materials.

- **Natural Materials**

The qualities of natural materials differ from the synthetic material and knowing these qualities would help you to make better use of them. Natural cord materials existing today include Jute, Hemp, Leather, Cotton, Silk and Flax. There are also yarns made from natural fibers. Natural material fibers are made from plants and animals.

- **Synthetic Materials**

Like natural materials, synthetic materials are also used in macramé projects. The fibers of synthetic materials are made through chemical processes. The major ones are nylon beading cord, olefin, satin cord, and parachute cord.

General Supplies

The Essential Project Board

There are several different kinds of padded board designs available on the internet. Some are made of foam and others of cork. There are also some available for purchase in bead stores that are not foam, but instead have a scalloped edge that allows you to wedge your cord in between the scallops, provided your cords are long enough to reach the edge of the board.

I prefer to use thick foam which gives me the ability to push my straight pin all the way in, using the head to hold the cord tightly when necessary. A feature I used often when I was first learning. I also often pin horizontally across a cord to give it some tension without piercing the cord itself.

To make my board, I started with a leftover piece of foam that was lying around. (Ok, it was lying around at my mom's house, but it was in the attic, so it is fair game, right?). As you can see, I made a rough cut that is a bit larger than my clip board. This is about 12in x 13in. Where the top clip will be, I cut out a slope.

I added about 4 inches to each side and cut out my fabric. Choose wisely here. On my first try, I used a very light, soft pink fabric that was a flannel type of material. When I worked on a project though, especially picking up beads to string onto the cords, I was forever having little bits of fluff on my fingers and in my way. Cotton is a better choice. Cover the foam with your fabric. Turn to the back and safety pin it in place. I like to be able to take the cover off to wash it (there may be a coffee spill in the future) or just change it out if it does not work (like the pink stuff).

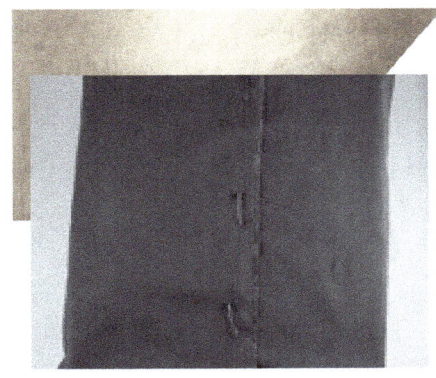

Turn to the front and fit onto your clipboard.

I keep straight pins in the top corners of my board, which I use to pin cords, hold the fastenings (closures), or keep a focal bead.

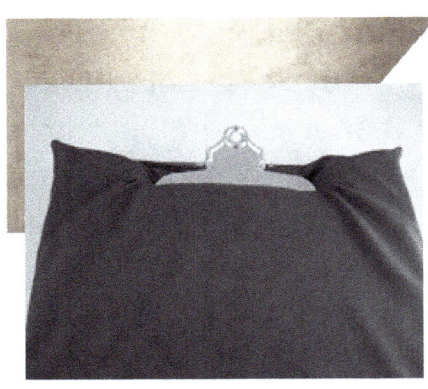

Reaming tools

Tools

The right beads can really complement your project. What fun it is finding the perfect shape and color, then rushing home to work it into your creation – and what disappointment if you then spend hours wrestling with the tiny bead opening which is stubbornly refusing to go on to your cord.

So, what is the solution? A simple set of bead reamers. I most often use the smallest one, but I have had occasion to reach for the subsequent size up also. My reamers are for use on glass, ceramic, pearl, and stone beads. This tool can literally smooth the way with tricky beads.

Beading tools

It is a good idea to have some basic beading tools on hand. Several patterns have jump rings or ribbon clasp closures, which would benefit from the use of (shown from left to right) needle nose pliers, round nose pliers, a crimp tool and wire cutters. You will also need a pair of small, sharp scissors. And I do mean sharp; if they are dull, they will

Glue

Often in micro-macramé, your only loose ends are at the end of the project when you tie it all off. In my experience, this is your weakest link. So why not strengthen it as best as you can? Many people use nail polish; I prefer glue. One type of glue you can use is E6000. It works well on leather and many jewelry makers prefer to use it.

Another good choice is Beacon 527 multi-purpose glue. It dries clear, though shiny. Usually I leave it to dry well (often overnight) then trim my cords and apply a second coat.

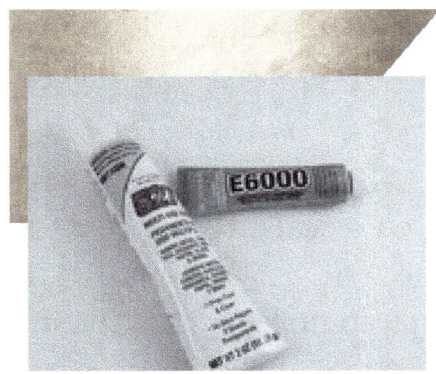

Note: Some crafters use a singeing tool to fuse the ends of nylon cords, melting them together. This leaves a bit of black residue, so use this technique only on dark cords, or where it will not show like behind a focal bead or button.

Pins

Straight pins are significant in micro-macramé design work. Some people prefer T-pins. Either way, a long

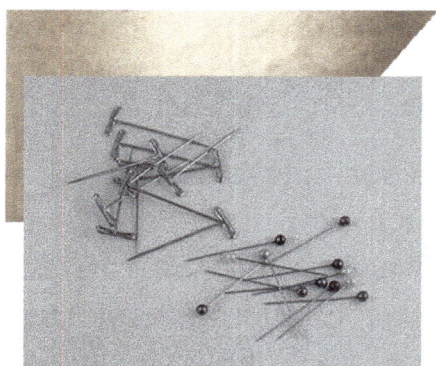

shank is more comfortable to work with. Pins are vital when it comes to holding cords in place, and useful for teasing out a mistake without unraveling your cord.

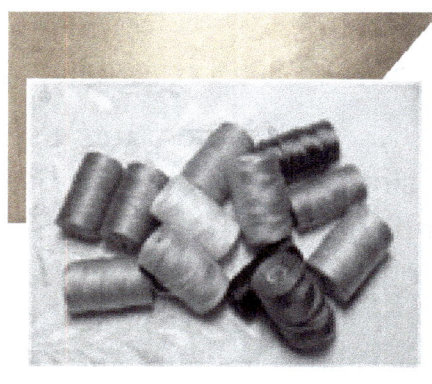

Cords and Beads

Types of cording

C-Lon - My patterns use a cord called C-Lon Bead Cord. It is a 3-ply nylon cord comparable to Conso and Mastex Nylon #18 but offers a much larger range of color options and a smaller price per spool. This cord is the standard size for micro macramé jewelry. It is also available in smaller diameters.

Tuff - Also a 3-ply nylon cord, it is available in 16 colors and has several size options. It does not stretch or stain, and resists fraying. Size 5 is comparable to C-Lon Beading Cord.

MACRAMÉ PROJECTS

D&E (formerly Mastex no. 18) – nylon cord originally designed for the upholstery industry, it is soft and pliable. Available in about 17 colors.

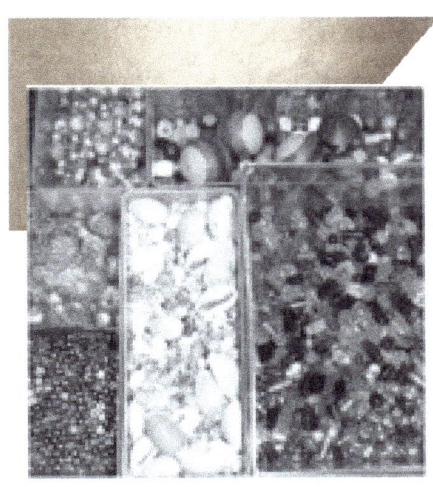

Types of beads

Metal – These are non-precious metals, which offer a less expensive alternative to silver and gold.

Crystal – It is the refraction created by the many cuts in a glass surface that gives crystal it is fancy shine.

Glass – This category is where you will find flame work and lamp work beads. Versatile and affordable, glass bead is an excellent choice for novice beaders.

Semiprecious (or gemstone) – These beads are a popular choice as they offer a large variety of options. The list is extensive, so here are a just a few: agate, amber, garnet, jade, malachite, and onyx.

Clay - These beads can be made of ceramic clay, which is fired in a kiln and glazed, or made of porcelain, which generally involves a potter's wheel, a kiln, and hand painting. There is also polymer clay, which is not technically a clay at all, but a plastic. This material is an oven-baked clay that can be used at home to make your own unique beads and is very versatile.

Other - There are also beads made from shell, such as mother of pearl, tiger shell, abalone, and conch shells. You may also come across wooden beads which come from the bark, roots, or branches of many types of trees. Some wooden beads are carved and have been popular for generations.

Cord Measurement

Before you can embark on a macramé project, it is essential that you determine the amount of chord you will need. This includes knowing the length of the required cord and the total number of materials you must purchase.

Equipment: to measure, you will need a paper for writing, pencil, tape rule and calculator. You would also need some basic knowledge of unit conversion as shared below:

> 1 inch = 25.4 millimeters = 2.54 centimeters
> 1 foot = 12 inches
> 1 yard = 3 feet = 36 inches
> 1 yard = 0.9 meters

Note: The circumference of a ring = 3.14 * diameter measured across the ring

Measuring Width

The first thing to do is determine the finished width

of the widest area of your project. Once you have this width, pencil it down.

Determine the actual size of the materials, by measuring its width from edge to edge.

You can then proceed to determine the type of knot pattern you wish to use with the knowledge of the knot pattern. You must know the width and spacing (if required) of each knot. You should also determine if you want to add more cords to widen an area of if you would be needing extra cords for damps.

With the formula given above, calculate and determine the circumference of the ring of your designs.

Determine the mounting technique to be used. The cord can be mounted to a dowel, ring, or other cord. Folded cords affect both the length and width of the cord measurement.

CHAPTER - 2
Knots and Techniques

Chinese Crown Knot

This is a great beginning knot for any project and can be used as the foundation for the base of the project. Use lightweight cord for this— it can be purchased at craft stores or online, wherever you get your macramé supplies.

Watch the photos very carefully as you move along with this project and take your time to make sure you are using the right string in the right point of the project.

Do not rush, and make sure you have even tension throughout. Practice makes perfect, but with the illustrations to help you, you will find It is not hard at all to create.

Use a pin to help keep everything in place as you are working.

Weave the strings in and out of each other as you can see in the photos. It helps to practice with different colors to help you see what is going on.

Pull the knot tight, then repeat for the row on the outside.

Continue to do this as often as you like to create the knot. You can make it as thick as you like, depending on the project. You can also create more than one length on the same cord.

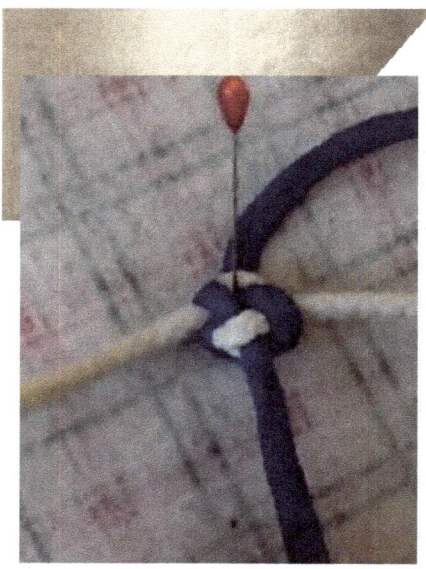

For the finished project, make sure that you have all your knots secure and firm throughout, and do your best to make sure it is all even. It is going to take practice before you can get it perfectly each time, but remember that practice does make perfect, and with time, you are going to get it without too much trouble.

Make sure all is even, secure and tie off. Snip off all the loose ends, and you are ready to go!

Square Knot

This is a great beginning knot for any project and can be used as the foundation for the base of the project. Use lightweight cord for this – it can be purchased at craft stores or online, wherever you get your macramé supplies.

MACRAMÉ PROJECTS

Watch the photos very carefully as you move along with this project and take your time to make sure you are using the right string in the right point of the project.

Do not rush, and make sure you have even tension throughout. Practice makes perfect, but with the illustrations to help you, you will find it is not hard at all to create.

For the finished project, make sure that you have all your knots secure and firm throughout, and do your best to make sure it is all even. It is going to take practice before you can get it perfectly each time, but remember that practice does make perfect, and with time, you are going to get it without too much trouble.

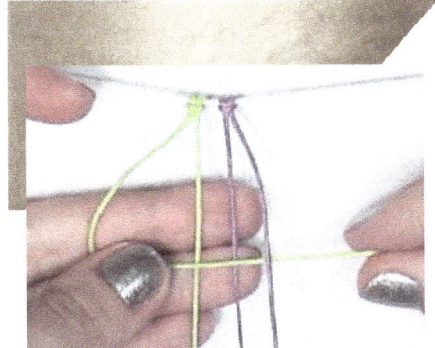

Make sure all is even, secure and tie off. Snip off all the loose ends, and you are ready to go!

Alternating Square Knots

This is the perfect knot to use for basket hangings, decorations, or any projects that are going to require you to put weight on the project. Use a heavier weight cord for this, which you can find at craft stores or online.

Watch the photos very carefully as you move along with this project and take your time to make sure you are using the right string in the right point of the project.

Do not rush, and make sure you have even tension throughout. Practice makes perfect, but with the illustrations to help you, you will find It is not hard at all to create.

Start at the top of the project and work your way toward the bottom. Keep it even as you work your way throughout the piece. Tie the knots at 4-inch intervals, working your way down the entire thing.

Tie each new knot securely before you move on to the one. Remember that the more even you get the better it is.

Work on one side of the piece first and then tie the knot on the other side. You are going to continue to alternate sides, with a knot joining them in the middle, as you can see in the photo.

Again, keep this even as you work throughout.

Bring the knot in toward the center and make sure you have even lengths on both sides of the piece.

Pull this securely up to the center of the cord, then move on to the on the cord.

MACRAMÉ PROJECTS

You are going to gather the cord on one side for the set of knots and then you are going to go back to the other side of the piece to work another set of knots on the other side.

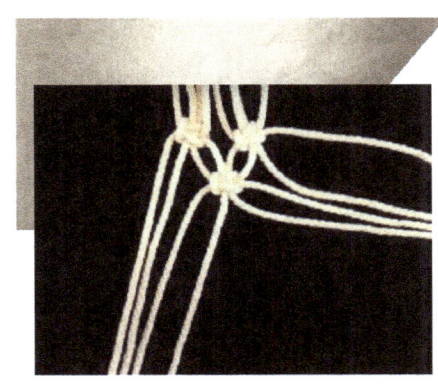

Work this evenly, then you are going to come back to the center.

It is a matter of sequence. Work the one side, then go back to the beginning, then go back to the other side once more.

Continue to do this for as long as your cords are, or if you need for the project.

For the finished project, make sure that you have all your knots secure and firm throughout, and do your best to make sure it is all even. It is going to take practice before you can get it perfectly each time, but remember that practice does make perfect, and with time, you are going to get it without too much trouble.

Make sure all is even, secure and tie off. Snip off all the loose ends, and you are ready to go!

Lark's Head Knot

This is a great beginning knot for any project and can be used as the foundation for the base of the project. Use lightweight cord for this – it can be purchased at craft stores or online, wherever you get your macramé supplies.

Watch the photos very carefully as you move along with this project and take your time to make sure you are using the right string in the right point of the project.

Do not rush, and make sure you have even tension throughout. Practice makes perfect, but with the illustrations to help you, you will find it is not hard at all to create.

Use the base string as the core part of the knot, working around the end of the string with the cord. Make sure all is even as you loop the string around the base of the cord.

Create a slip knot around the base of the string and keep both ends even as you pull the cord through the center of the piece.

For the finished project, make sure that you have all your knots secure and firm throughout, and do your best to make sure it is all even. It is going to take practice before you can get it perfectly each time, but remember that practice does make perfect, and with time, you are going to get it without too much trouble.

Make sure all is even, secure and tie off. Snip off all the loose ends, and you are ready to go!

Reverse Lark's Head Knot

This is a great beginning knot for any project and can be used as the foundation for the base of the project.

Use lightweight cord for this – it can be purchased at craft stores or online, wherever you get your macramé supplies.

Watch the photos very carefully as you move along with this project and take your time to make sure you are using the right string in the right point of the project.

Do not rush, and make sure you have even tension throughout. Practice makes perfect, but with the illustrations to help you, you will find It is not hard at all to create.

Use two hands to make sure that you have everything even and tight as you work. You can use tweezers if it helps to make it tight against the base of the string.

Use both hands to pull the string evenly down against the base string to create the knot.

Again, keep the base even as you pull the center, creating the firm knot against your guide cord.

For the finished project, make sure that you have all your knots secure and firm throughout, and do your best to make sure it is all even. It is going to take practice before you can get it perfectly each time, but remember that practice does make perfect, and with time, you are going to get it without too much trouble.

Make sure all is even, secure and tie off. Snip off all the loose ends, and you are ready to go!

CHAPTER - 3
Macramé Pillows, Dream Catcher Plus Wrapping Techniques

Project 1: Macramé Fringe Tassel Pillow:

Materials:

Plain cloth zipper pillow covers in the components of your pillow insert. A combination of enriching fringe trim (I discovered mine at yard sales, however you can find some comparable here or there), Measuring stick, Texture scissors, Launderable texture pen, Texture Glue (I used Liquid Stitch and Brawl Check).

I spread out my plain pillow cover. I most likely could have pressed it first, however I am not excessively that kind of young lady. At that point I cut my first line of fringe trim to be the specific width of the pillowcase. No estimating fundamental! Simply line it up and cut!

Spread out and cut the remainder of your columns of trim to length, and invest some energy adjusting them until you get them exactly how you need them on the completed item! Make little checks on the edges of where your line of paste will be, that way when you flush out the fringe trim, you can use your measuring stick (or anything with a straight edge) to draw an obvious conclusion and make a straight line over... with your texture stamping pen (or then again if you are like me, you can use your child's Crayola marker since it is advantageously inside arms reach and it will be covered by fringe at any rate).

Fringe pillow instructional exercise:

Make certain to follow all the instructions on your texture stick (I used Liquid Stitch) and press out an even bit of glue across one of your pen lines. At that point start toward one side and carefully push down the fringe trim as you go. It is alright if it does not go down great since you have a chance to straighten it out before the glue dries. Note! Of COURSE, you can use a sewing machine rather than texture stick for this, however I simply would not like to upset attempting to control the pillow cover so that I was not sewing through the two layers. You may be a more skilled needle worker than me however, so put it all on the line!

Stay back and ensure it's straight and in any event, changing is essential. At that point stick down the remainder of your columns in a similar way! Rehash these means on the other side of your cover, so they reflect one another. Also, use the Fray Check on the edges to keep your trim from fraying!

This texture sticks dries to the touch very quickly; however, I gave it a decent 24 hours before I upset it as a sanity check. I made two of these at a time, since

I needed to take a stab at destroying one of them just to see how things were made! The main time I used Rit Dye was on this undertaking, so I am a sorry ace and was somewhat threatened that I would destroy it. Be that as it may, I think it turned out great! (The color I used was blue green).

If I had let it soak longer, I am speculating the fringe would have gotten darker and been nearer to a similar color as the cloth, yet I would not fret this monochromatic looks great as well! In case you are intending to color yours, I suggest passing on the fringe and pillow cover independently before you fasten the fringe trim to the pillow.

Project 2: Gift Wrap

DIY macramé blessing wrap might be the simplest method to jump on the macramé train. Or possibly it was for me. I needed to take a stab at the specialty, however, I realized that hopping into a gigantic venture could end in calamity. Here is my method for taking a stab at the macramé knots…. All at once! Simply use them to enliven your bundles and you have DIY macramé blessing wrap. Magnificent right? This one was originally posted over at Crafts Unleashed where I am a plan colleague. I am posting it here on the off chance that you missed it! Add this macramé blessing wrap to any blessing that you are giving! A brisk and simple specialty thought!

At that point simply put in a couple of more days idealizing your procedures and adding to your skill level. In a little while you will have a stunning macramé wall hanging in your home!

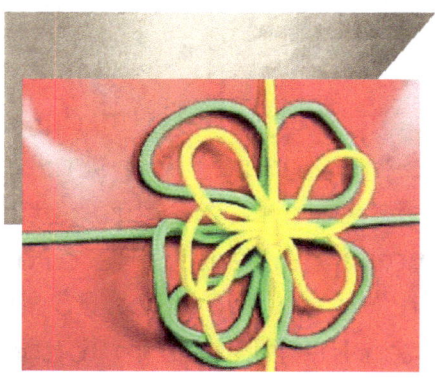

Project 3: Dream Catcher

Step 1 - First we will create the dream catcher center piece for the bracelet.

Push the 6mm hematite bead into the center of the wire shape and move the

MACRAMÉ PROJECTS

wire wraps over and around it to secure it in place.

Step 2 - Cut a 5cm length of 6mm wire.

Make a small loop in one end of the wire using the ends of the round nosed pliers. Thread on 4mm hematite bead onto the wire.

Step 3 - Make a second small loop to match the first, after the hematite bead. Trim off any excess wire as needed.

Step 4 - Create two more hematite bead components to match the one created in steps 2 and 3.

Step 5 - Using 3 4mm jump rings attach the feathers to one loop on each hematite bead component.

Step 6 - Attach 3 further 4mm jump rings to the opposite ends of the hematite bead component. These will be the dream catcher tails.

Step 7 - Use the last 3 4mm jump rings to connect the tails to the wrapped wire shape. You may find it easier to use both pairs of pliers to close the jump rings in this step.

Step 8 - Gently heat the ends of all the rattail cords to seal them and prevent fraying.

Using a lark's head knot, attach one of the 40-inch cord to the center of one side of the dream catcher.

A lark's head knot is created by folding the cord in half and then threading the loop created in the middle over the rim of the dream catcher. The long cord ends are then threaded through the loop and pulled until the loop closes around the metal rim.

The loop can be threaded through in either direction, but you will need to do all three the same way as doing so front to back creates a knot that looks different to threading the cord back to front.

MACRAMÉ PROJECTS

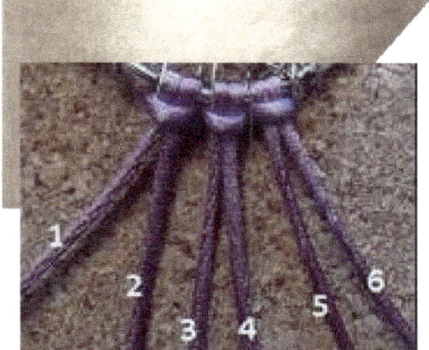

Step 9 - Attach the other two 40-inch cords to the dream catcher in the same way, one of each side of the first.

Step 10 - Spread out the cords and mentally number them from 1 to 6.

Step 11 -. Thread one 8mm hematite bead onto thread 2. Using threads 1 and 3 tie one square knot underneath the bead.

Step 12 - Thread one 8mm hematite bead onto thread 5. Using threads 4 and 6 tie one square knot underneath the bead.

Step 13- Separate the cords out so that cord 1 and 6 are laid out to the side, cords 3 and 4 are straight down in the center and cords 2 and 5 are in between.

Step 14 - Using cords 2 and 5 tie two square knots around cords 3 and 4.

Step 15 - Separate the cords into two sets of three. Thread an 8mm hematite bead onto cord 1. Using cords 1 and 3 and tie one square knot around cord 2.

Step 16 - Repeat step 15 using the second set of three cords. The bead is threaded onto cord 6 and then cords 4 and 6 are used to tie a square knot around cord 5.

Steps 11 to 16 form the bracelets pattern.

Step 17 - Repeat steps 11 - 16 once one so that there are four rows of beads.

Step 18 - Use cords 1 and 6 to tie a square knot around the four remaining cords.

Step 19 - Carefully cut off the remaining lengths of cords 2 and 5 leaving a 3mm tail. Gently heat the ends so they melt slightly. Press this melted end against the two remaining central cords (cords 3 and 4). Take your time completing this step so not to damage any of the other cords.

The melted end of the rat tail cord gets quite hot and can stick to skin so it best to use the point of your scissors or a needle to complete this step.

Step 20 - Tie another square knot directly below the previous knot.

Step 21 - Measure down 1.5 inches and fold the central rattail cords in half.

Step 22 - Hold the central cords between two fingers at the point where they meet the square knots and trim off the excess cord. Gently heat the edges to stop them fraying.

Step 23 - Tie a square knot around the folded over cords to hold the in place.

This creates a loop that will become part of the bracelet's fastener.

MACRAMÉ PROJECTS 41

Pull this knot tight.

Step 24 - Continue tying square knots until there is only 1 cm of the loop left showing.

This loop needs to be sized so that it is a tight fit for the disk bead to fit through. Test with your bead and adjust as needed before moving on to step 25.

Step 25 - Cut off the excess cords leaving a 3mm tail. Gently heat the ends so they melt slightly. Press this melted end against the final square knot. Take care completing this step so not to damage any of the other cords.

The melted end of the rat tail cord gets quite hot and can stick to skin so it best to use the point of your scissors or a needle to complete this step.

Step 26 - Repeat steps 8 and 9 to attach the three 20 lengths of rattail cord to the opposite side of the dream catcher.

Take care to form the lark's heads knot the same as you did on the other side.

Step 27- Repeat steps 10 - 16 to create a section of hematite beads to match the one already created.

Step 28 - Use cords 1 and 6 to tie a square knot around the four remaining cords.

Step 29 - Carefully cut off the remaining lengths of cords 2 and 5 leaving a 3mm tail. Gently heat the ends so they melt slightly. Press this melted end against the two remaining central cords (cords 3 and 4). Take care completing this step so not to damage any of the other cords.

The melted end of the rat tail cord gets quite hot and can stick to skin so it best to use the point of your scissors or a needle to complete this step.

Step 30- Tie another square knot directly below the previous knot.

Step 31 - Continue tying square knots until you have a Sennett measuring 2cm long.

Step 32- Trim off the excess knotting cords leaving a 3mm tail. Gently heat the ends so they melt slightly. Press this melted end against the two remaining central cords (cords 3 and 4).

Take your time completing this step so not to damage any of the other cords.

The melted end of the rat tail cord gets quite hot

and can stick to skin so it best to use the point of your scissors or a needle to complete this step.

Step 33 - Now trim off one of the central cords in the same way as described in step 32.

Step 34 - Thread the hematite disk bead on the remaining central cord.

Step 35- Leave a 3mm gap between the final square knot and the bead, tie one overhand knot to secure it on the cord.

Step 36 - Trim off the remaining cord and melt the end to prevent fraying.

CHAPTER - 4
Macramé Bracelets I

Project 4: Macramé Bracelet with Rattail Cord and Glass Beads

This tutorial provides step-by-step instructions with photos showing you how to create a simple beaded macramé bracelet with rattail cord and glass beads. This is a great tutorial for beginners, as it only requires knowing how to tie a half knot to complete.

Colors and beads can be substituted to suit personal tastes.

Materials List:

130cm length of 1mm rattail cord

1 10-12mm disk bead or button with central hole (hole must be 1mm minimum)

10 6mm black glass spacer beads

3 6mm patterned glass spacer beads

Tools List:

Macramé board and pins (optional)

Ruler

Scissors

Lighter

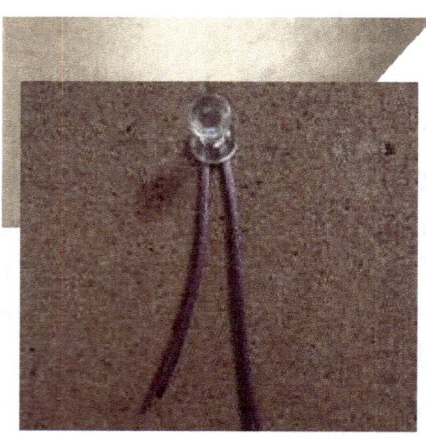

Step 1 - Fold over the first 5cm of the shorter length of cord and lay in front of you. These are the central cords.

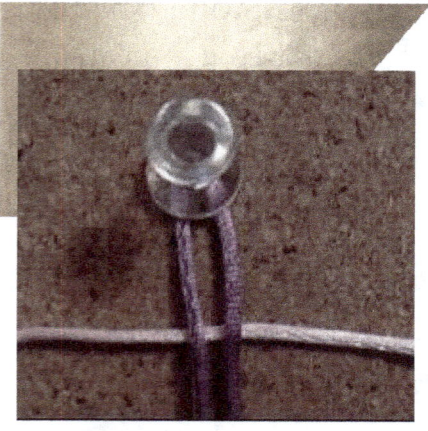

Step 2 - Fold the longer cord in half and place the center point underneath both cords.

MACRAMÉ PROJECTS

Step 3 - Starting with the left side cord tie one half knot.

Step 4 - Tighten the knot fully and position it to create a 10mm loop in the end of the shorter length of cord. This loop will form part of the bracelets fastener and needs to be a tight fit for the disk bead to fit through. Adjust as needed to suit your bead.

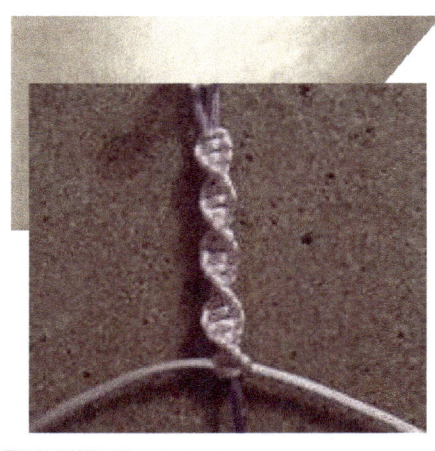

Step 5 - Always starting with the left side knotting cord, continue tying half knots until you have a Sennett 3.5cm long. The Spiral pattern can be seen forming within a few knots. Pull the first few knots tied a little tighter than normal to hold the loop created in step 1 securely. The completed section of bracelet, including the loop should measure approximately 4.5cm.

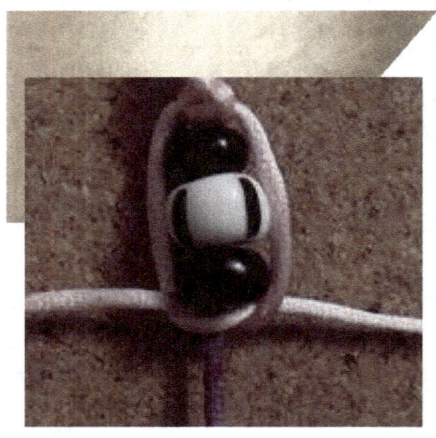

Step 6 - Thread one black bead, a patterned bead and a second black bead onto the central cord and move these up to the bottom of the knots. Tie one half knot underneath the beads to hold them in place. This knot should not to too tight. The beads should be sitting freely with the cords around them not squashed together.

Step 7 - Tie a further four half knots.

MACRAMÉ PROJECTS

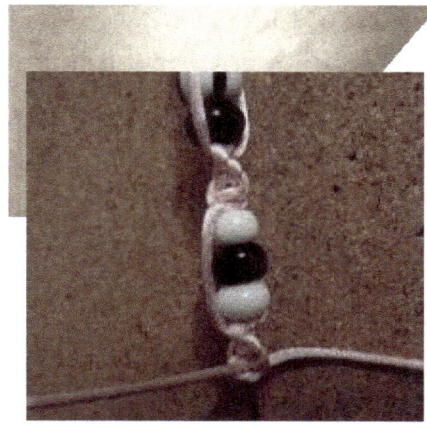

Step 8 - Repeat step 6, this time adding one white, one black and then a second black bead. Tie four more half knots.

Step 9 - Repeat steps 6-8 until all the beads have been added to the bracelet.

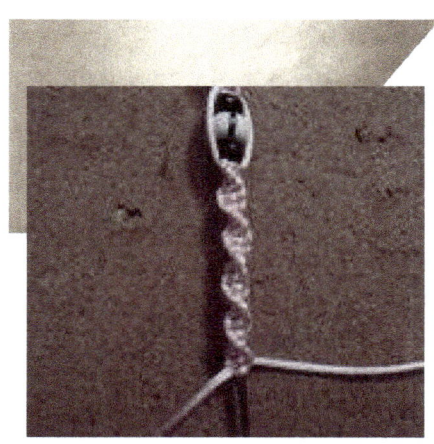

Step 10 - Continue tying half knots until you have a 3.5 cm Sennett to match the one at the beginning of the bracelet.

Step 11 - Cut off the excess knotting cords leaving a 3mm tail. Gently melt this tail using the lighter and fuse them to the final knot.

The melted rattail cord can get very hot and stick to skin so it is best to use the point of the scissors, a needle or similar item to carry out this step.

Step 12 - Thread the disk bead on to the central cord. Leave a gap of 3mm between the last knot and the bead and tie an overhand knot to secure the bead. Trim of the excess central cord and gently melt the end to prevent fraying.

Project 5: Black and Red Macramé Bracelet

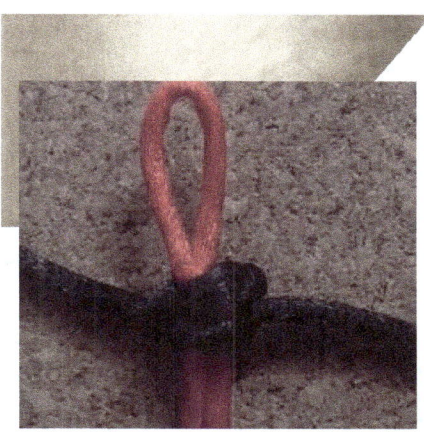

Step 1 - Fold the shorter red cord in half and lay it flat in front of you. These are the designs central cords.

Step 2 - Fold the black cord in half and tie one square knot around the red central cords.

This knot needs to be positioned so that it creates a loop that the bead/flat button can pass through tightly. This forms the bracelets fastener.

Step 3 - Fold the longer red rattail cord in half and tie one half knot around the red central cords underneath the black square knot.

 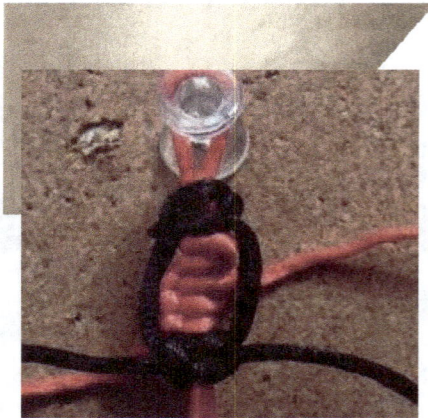

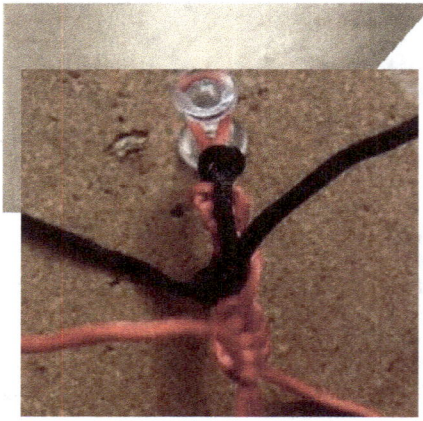

Step 4 - Tie a further four half knots always starting with the same side cord so that the knots begin to form a spiral.

Step 5 - Carry the black cords over the red and tie one square knot underneath the half knots.

Step 6 - Pass the red cords under the black and tie five half knots.

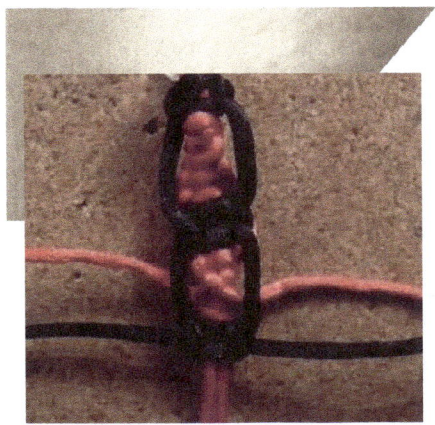 

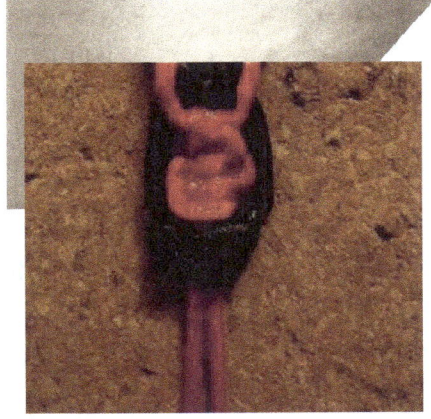

Step 7 - Continue in this way until you have tied 18cm of knots.

If you have the bracelet pinned to a board or solid surface, the bracelet will twist as the spirals forms so you may find it easier to unpin and re-pin it as you work. The black cords should be flat, only the red knotting cords form the spiral.

Step 8 - Turn the bracelet over and trim away all the excess knotting cords leaving 3mm ends.

Step 9 - Gently melt the cord end with the lighter and press them against the knots.

Heated rattail cord becomes very hot and can stick to your skin and burn so this step is safest carries out using a needle or scissors point to press on the melting cord.

Step 10 - Thread the flat bead/button onto the central cords. Push it up to the knots and leaving a 3mm gap tie an overhand knot to secure the bead. Cut off any excess cord and gently melt the ends to prevent fraying.

Project 6: Fish Bone Macramé Bracelet

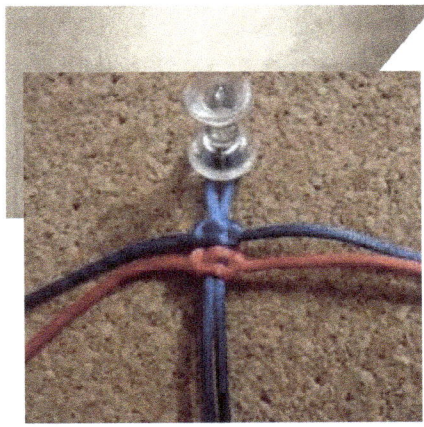

Step 1 - Fold the shorter blue cord in half and lay it in front of you.

Step 2 - Fold the long blue cord in half and tie one square knot around the shorter cord.

This knot should be positioned so that the loop created is a tight fit for the bead/button to fit through.

Step 3 - Use the red cord to tie a square knot underneath the bead.

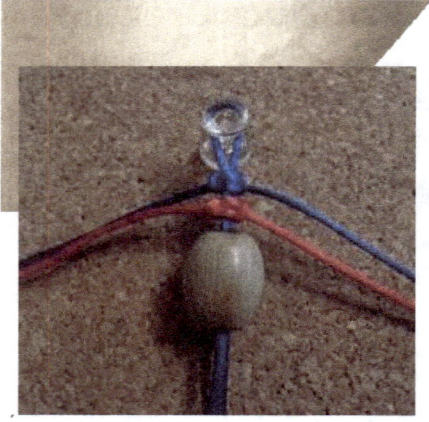

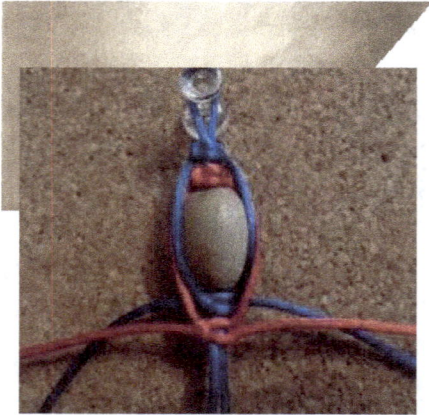

Step 4 – Place a thread on the first bead.

Step 5 - Carry the blue cords over the red and tie a square knot underneath the bead.

Step 6 - Carry the red cords over and tie a square knot underneath the blue knot.

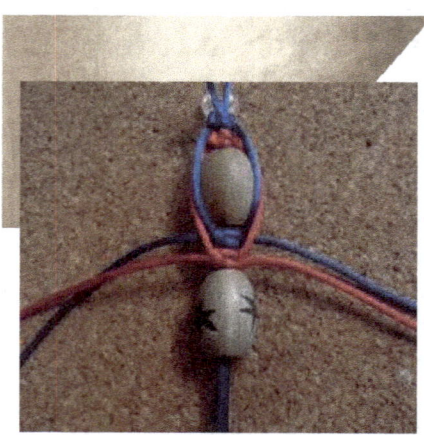

Step 7 – Place a thread on a second bead.

Step 8 - Repeat steps 5 and 6.

Step 9 - Continue in this way until all the beads have been added.

Step 10 - Leaving a 3mm tail cut off the remaining knotting cord on one side. Use the lighter to melt the ends and stick them to the back of the knots.

Take care with the melting cord as it gets very hot and can stick to your skin and burn. Use a needle or point of the scissors to press down the cord.

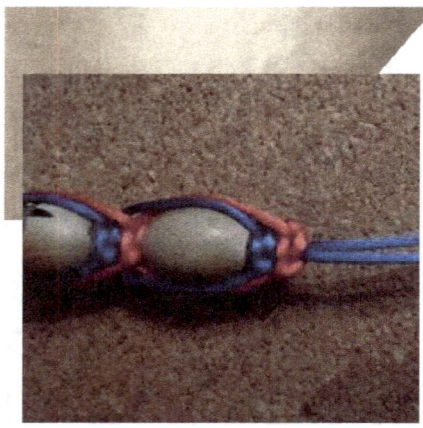

Step 11 - Repeat step 10 with the remaining cords.

Step 12 – Place a thread on the disk bead/button. Leave a 3mm gap

between the final knot and the bead and tie an overhand knot.

Cut off any excess cord and melt the ends to prevent fraying.

Project 7: Side by Side Macramé Bracelet

Step 1 - Gently heat the ends of each cord to make it easier to thread on the beads and prevent fraying.

Fold one cord in half and secure to your macramé board (if using).

Step 2 - Fold a second cord in half and use it to tie one square knot around the cords on the macramé board.

Position this knot to create a small loop in the end of the first cord. This loop should be sized so that the flat bead/button fits through with a little pressure.

Step 3 - Fold the final length of cord in half and use it to tie one square knot underneath the knot tied in step 2.

You should now have six cords, grouped in three sets of two.

Step 4 - Regroup the cords into two sets of three.

Step 5 - Working with one set of three cords, thread one bead purple and one silver bead on to the outer cords.

Step 6 - Using these two outer cords, tie one square knot around the central cord below the beads.

Step 7 - Thread two more beads on to the outer cords and place them below the two already added to the bracelet.

Tie one square knot around the central cord below the beads.

Step 8 - Repeat step 7 until all the purple and silver beads have been added to the bracelet.

Step 9 - Return to the beginning of the bracelet. Thread the cord nearest to the row of silver beads through the first silver bead.

Step 10 - Thread one lilac bead onto the first cord in the set of three. This is the cord furthest from the beads.

Step 11 - Position this bead in line with the beads already added to the bracelet and tie one square knot beneath it.

Step 12 -. Thread the cord through the second silver bead. Add one lilac bead to the first cord and tie one square knot underneath it.

Step 13 - Repeat step 12 to add the lilac beads to the bracelet.

Step 14 - Separate the cords into three sets of two again.

Step 15 - Use the four outer cords to tie two square knots around the two central cords.

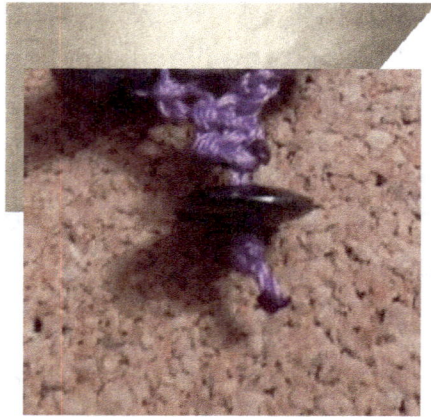

Step 16 - Turn the bracelet over and trim of the two sets of outer cords, leaving a 3mm tail.

Step 17 - Gently melt the cord ends and fuse them to the back of the knot.

Take care with this step as the melting cord is hot and can stick to your skin.

The point of the scissors can be used to press it into play.

Step 18 - Thread the disk bead/button onto the remaining two cords. Leaving a gap of 2mm between the last square knot and the bead, tie an overhand knot to secure. Trim of any excess cord and gently heat the end to prevent it fraying.

CHAPTER - 5
MACRAMÉ BRACELETS II

Project 8: Cross Choker

Step 1 - Fold over the first 1.5 inches if the shorter length of rattail cord. This will be used to create a loop as part of the bracelets fastening.

Step 2 - Fold the longer length of cord in half. Place the center point underneath the shorter cord and tie one square knot. These will be your knotting cords. This knot needs to be positioned so that it creates a loop in the end of the shorter cord that the disk bead can fit through with some pressure. If the

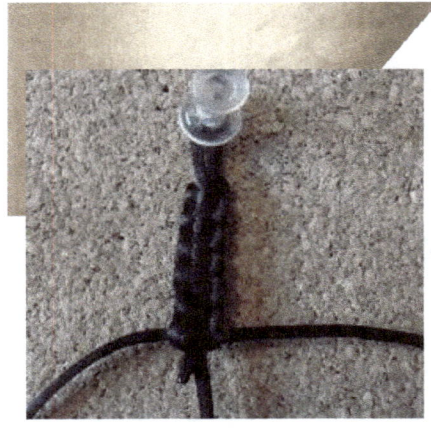

bead slides through too easily there is a possibility that the bracelet could come unfastened.

Step 3 - Tie a further five square knots.

Pull each knot tight as these are holding the two lengths of cord together.

Step 4 - Continue tying square knots until you have a Sennett 5.5 inches long.

Step 5 - Thread one silver foil bead on to the central cord.

Step 6 - Bring the knotting cords around the bead and tie one square knot.

Step 7 - Now thread on one cross charm and push it up to the last square knot. Because of the hole positioning the cross will not lay flat

Step 8 - Tie another square knot around the cross top.

Step 9 - Continue with steps 5 - 8 until all the beads and crosses have been added.

MACRAMÉ PROJECTS

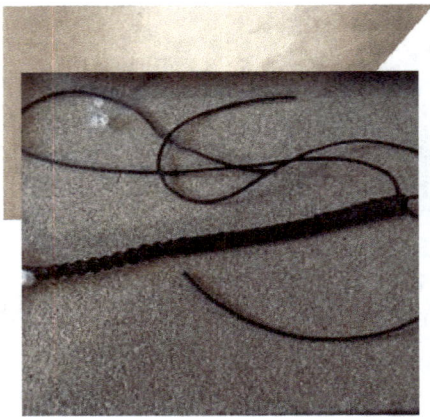

Step 10 - Now tie another Sennett of square knots 5.5 inches long.

Step 11 - Leaving a 3mm tail cut of the excess knotting cords. Using the lighter gently melt the ends and press them on to the square knots.

Care needs to be taken with this step as the melted cord can get very hot and stick to skin and burn. It is best to use a needle or scissor point to press down the cord.

Step 12 - Thread the disk bead (or button) on to the remaining cord.

Step 13 - Leaving a 3mm gap tie an overhand knot to secure the bead.

Step 14 - Cut of the excess cord and heat the ends gently with the lighter to seal and

prevent fraying.

Project 9: Macramé Beaded Wave Bracelets

Step 1 - Fold over the first 2 inches of the shorter length of waxed cotton cord.

Step 2 - Fold one of the long lengths of waxed cord in half. Place the half-way point underneath the shorter cord and tie one square knot around both cords.

Position the knot so that the loop created is a tight fit for the 12mm bead/button to fit through.

Step 3 - Fold a second longer length of cord in half and tie one square knot as in step one, directing under the existing knot.

MACRAMÉ PROJECTS

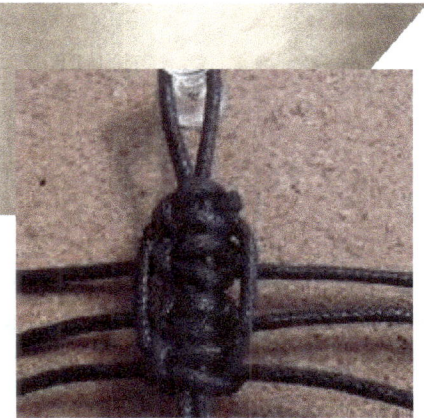

Step 4 - Repeat step 3 with the final length of waxed cord. Tighten each of these knots as they are holding the bracelets fastener secure and if they are loosed it may work itself undone with wear.

Step 5 - Arrange the cords so they are laying out to the sides of your central cord. Carry the first pair of cords over the others and tie one square knot underneath the set of three knots previously tied.

Step 6 - Repeat step 5 using the second pair of cords.

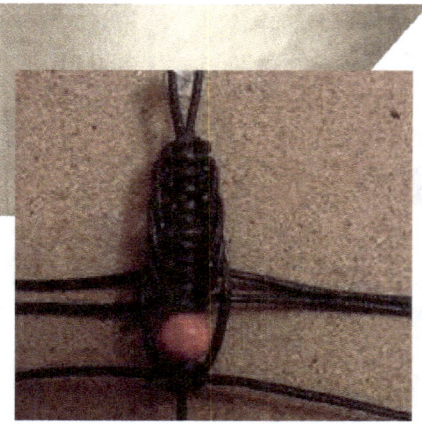
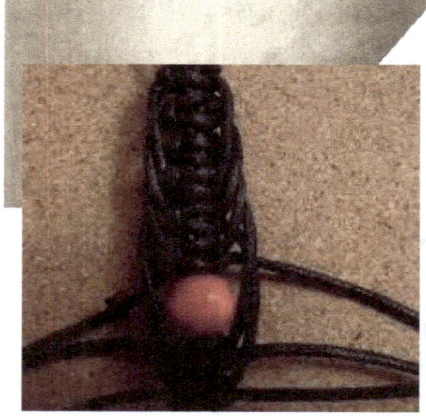

Step 7 - Finally repeat step 5 again with the third set of cords.

Step 8 - Thread one 8mm bead onto the central cord. Carry the first set of cords over the others and tie one square knot underneath the bead.

Step 9 - Carry the second set of cords over the others and tie one square knot underneath under the knot created in step 8.

MACRAMÉ PROJECTS

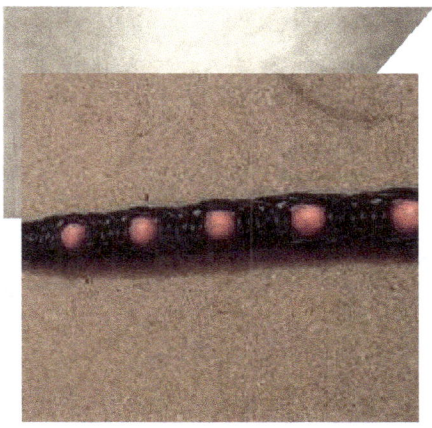

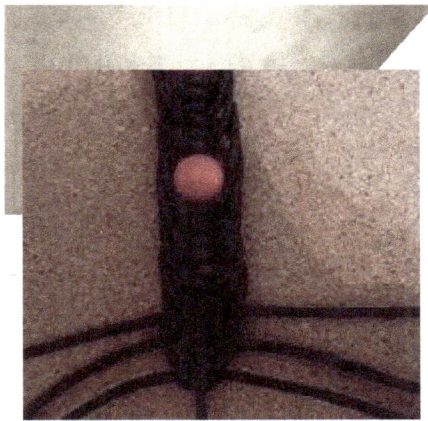

Step 10 - Repeat step 9 using the third set of cords.

Step 11 - Repeat steps 8 to 10 until you have added all five beads to the bracelet. Take care to always carry the cords over each other to keep the pattern continuous.

The bracelet length can be adjusted by adding or removing beads or by tying square knots at the beginning and end of the bracelet.

Step 12 - Repeat steps 5 - 7 so you have six square knots after the fifth bead.

MACRAMÉ PROJECTS

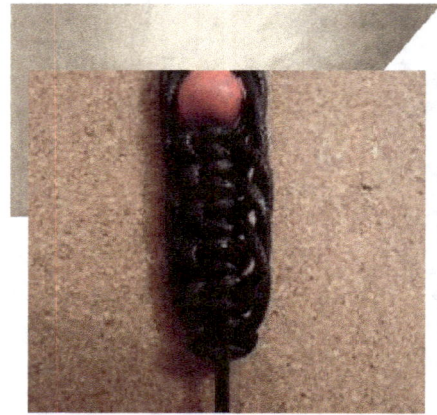

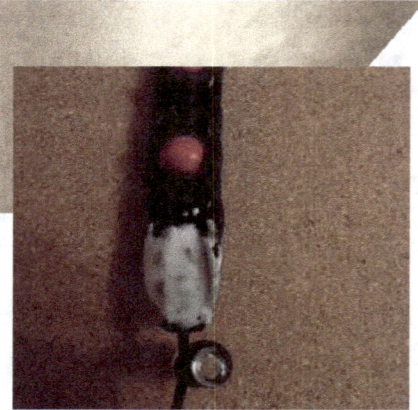

Step 13 - Pull the cords to tighten the final knots and then cut off the remaining cord.

Step 14 - Cover the cord ends and the surrounding area in PVA glue and allow to dry.

Step 15 - Thread the 12mm bead/button onto the central cord.

Project 10: Rainbow Bows Macramé Bracelet

Step 1 - Fold over the first 3cm on the shorter cord and secure it to your macramé board (if using) or lay it flat in front of you.

Step 2 - Fold in half the longer length of cord and tie one square knot around the cords. These will be your knotting cords.

Position the knot so that the loop created is sized to snugly fit the disk bead/button through. This loop forms part of the bracelets fastener and if it is too big, the bracelet may come unfastened.

Step 3 - Tie a further four-square knot.

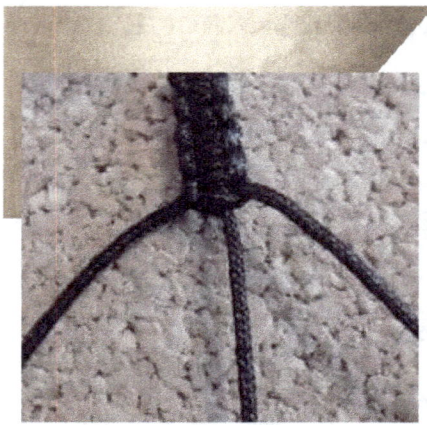 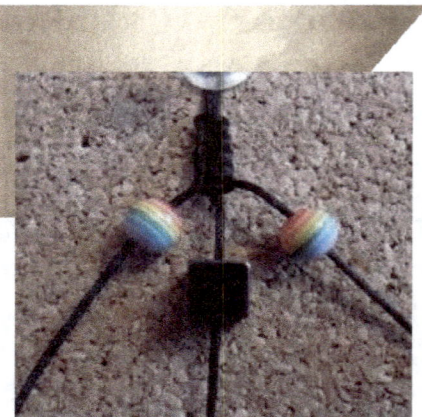

Step 4 - Very carefully trim off the short central cord.

Step 5 - Now begin added beads to the bracelet. To do this thread one hematite cube bead on to the central cord and one rainbow bead on to each of the knotting (side) cords.

Step 6 - Tie one square knot underneath the cube bead and

maneuver the beads into place as you do.

Step 7 - Continue adding beads in this way (steps 5 and 6) until they all been knotted into the bracelet.

Take care to keep the rainbow beads all the same way up. So, if the first beads have the red stripe first, keep them all this way up as this will lead to a neater and more fluid finished look.

Step 8 - Tie four square knots so you have five in total.

Step 9 - Turn the bracelet over and trim of the excess knotting cords, leaving a 3mm tail.

Step 10 - Using the lighter gently melt the cord ends and press them against the back of the bracelet to seal.

Take care with this step as the cord can get very hot and burn. The point of the scissors can be used to press the ends down.

Step 11 - Thread the disk bead/button onto the central cord. Leave a 3mm gap between the bead and the square knots and tie one overhand knot to secure.

Step 12 -. Use the lighter to gently melt the cord ends and fuse them to the final square knot.

Take care completing this step as the cord will get hot and can stick to your stick and burn. Use the scissors or a needle to press the cords down.

MACRAMÉ PROJECTS

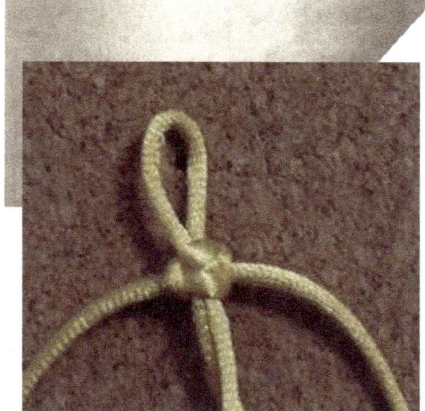

Project 11: Beaded Half Macramé Bracelet

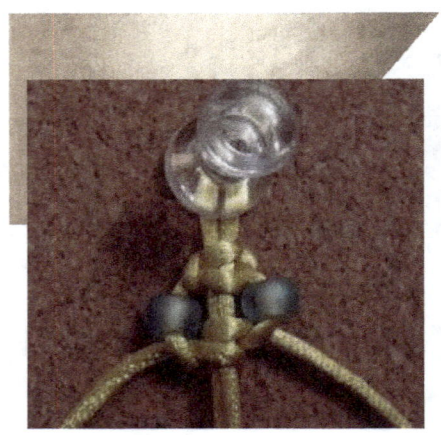
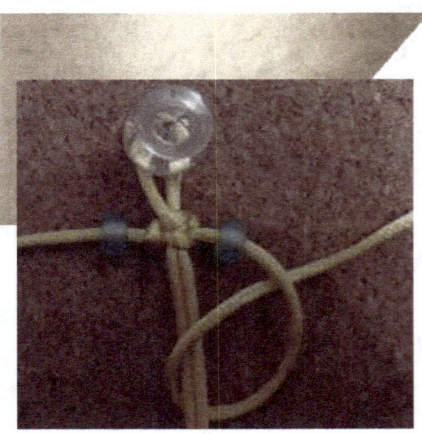

Step 1 - Gently melt the rattail cord ends. This stop fraying and makes it easier to thread the beads on.

Fold in half the 20-inch length of rattail and lay it flat in front of you. This will be your central cords.

Step 2 - Fold the long length of cord in half and place the center point underneath the shorter cord. This will be your knotting cords.

Step 3 - 1 cm from the top of the cord loop tie one square knot.

This knot needs to be placed so that the flat bead fits through the loop but is a tight fit.

Step 4 - Thread one frosted capri blue bead onto

each of the yellow knotting cords and push them up to the square knot tied in step 3.

Step 5 - Using the right-side cord tie one half hitch knot and pull tight.

Step 6 - Now use the left side cord to tie one half hitch knot underneath the first.

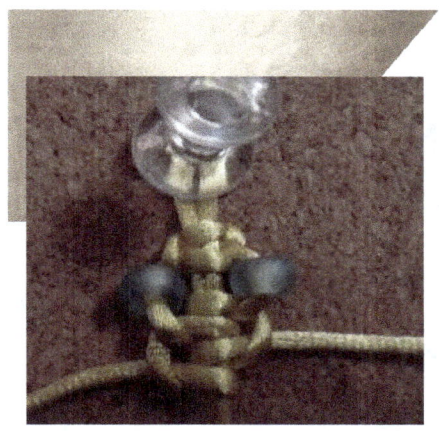

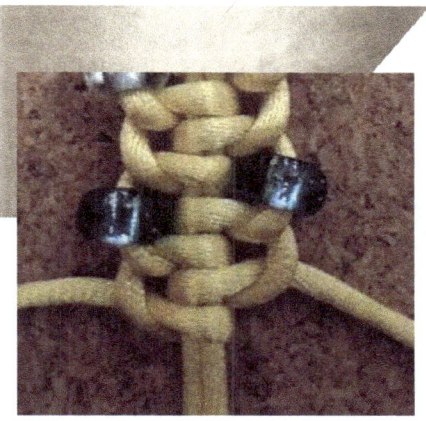

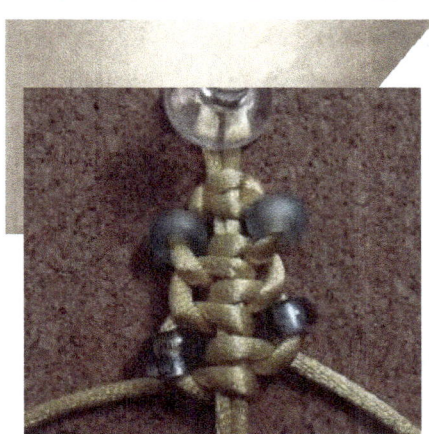

Step 7 - Tie one half hitch knot with each cord starting with the right side.

Step 8 - Thread one blue lined bead on to each cord.

Step 9 - Tie a set of half hitch knots, first using the right cord and then the left.

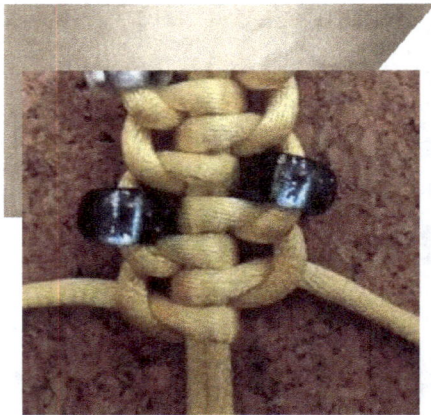
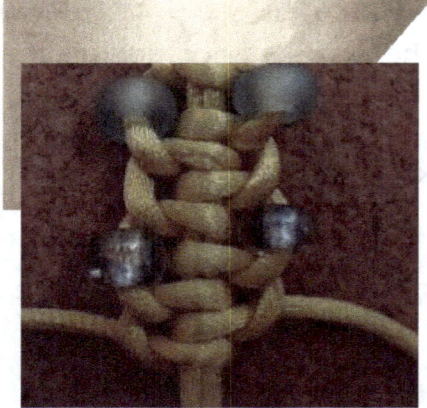

Step 10 - Tie one half hitch knot with each cord starting with the right side.

Step 11 - Repeat step 8 - 10, this time using the silver lined sapphire beads.

Step 12 - Finally repeat steps 8 - 10 using the frosted dark blue beads.

Continue adding beads in this way until all the beads have been added. The bracelet will measure approx. 7.5 inches long.

Bead order: Frosted cobalt blue, blue lined, silver lined sapphire and then frosted dark blue.

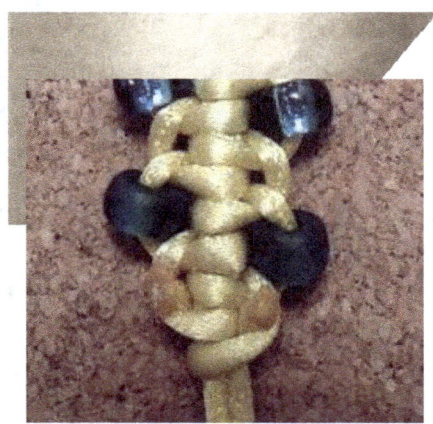 

Step 13 - Trim the two knotting cords leaving a 3mm end.

Using the lighter gently melt the cord ends and fuse them to the back of the bracelet.

Do not put the cord into the flame or it will burn and discolor, just hold it close. The melted cord is very hot and can stick to your skin and burn so it is safer to use a needle, scissors point of like press them down on the bracelet.

Step 14 - Thread the flat bead onto the two central cords and leaving a 3mm gap between the bead and the final half hitch knot, secure it using an overhand knot.

Cut off the excess central cords and melt the end to prevent it fraying.

CHAPTER - 6
Macramé Bracelets III

Project 12: Serenity Bracelet

(Note: if you are familiar with the flat knot, you can move right along into the next pattern)

This novice bracelet offers plenty of practice using one of micro Macramé most used knots. You will also gain experience in beading and equalizing tension. This bracelet features a button closure and the finished length is 7 inches.

Knots Used:

- Flat Knot (aka square knot)
- Overhand knot

Supplies:

- White C-Lon cord, 6 ½ ft, x 3
- 18 - Frosted Purple size 6 beads
- 36 - Purple seed beads, size 11
- 1 - 1 cm Purple and white focal bead
- 26 - Dark Purple size 6 beads
- 1 - 5 mm Purple button closure bead

(Note: the button bead needs to be able to fit onto all 6 cords)

Instructions:

Take all 3 cords and fold them in half. Find the center and place on your work surface as shown:

Now hold the cords and tie an overhand knot, loosely, at the center point. It should look like this:

MACRAMÉ PROJECTS

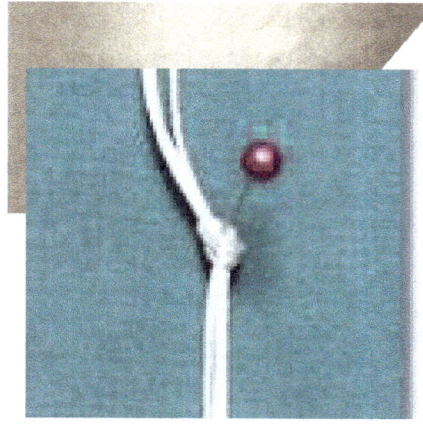

1. We will now make a buttonhole closure. Just below the knot, take each outer cord and tie a flat knot (aka square knot). Continue tying flat knots until you have about 2 ½ cm.

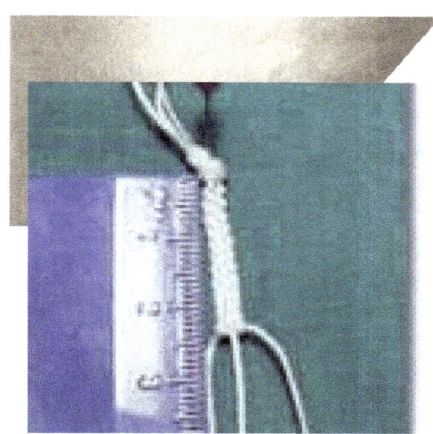

2. Undo your overhand knot and place the ends together in a horseshoe shape.

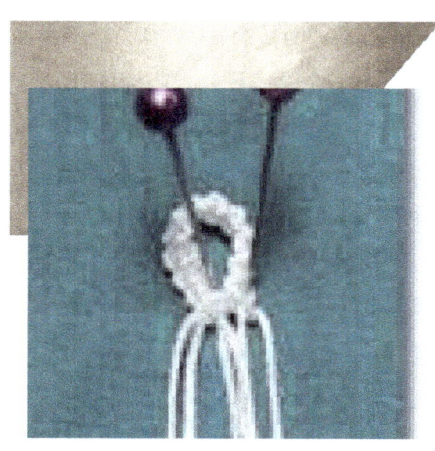

3. We now have all 6 cords together. Think of the cords as numbered 1 through 6 from left to right. Cords 2-5 will stay in the middle as filler cords. Find cord 1 and 6 and

use these to tie flat knots around the filler cords. (Note: now you can pass your button bead through the opening to ensure a good fit. Add or subtract flat knots as needed to create a snug fit. This size should be fine for a 5mm bead). Continue to tie flat knots until you have 4 cm length (to increase bracelet length, add more flat knots here, and the equal amount in step 10).

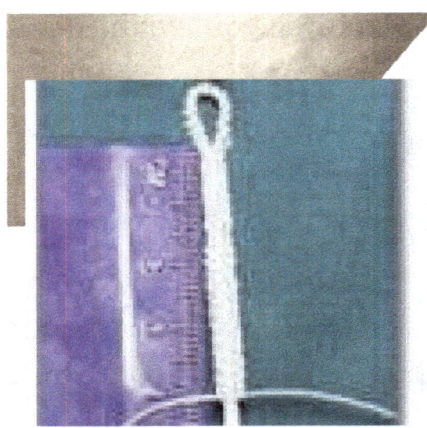

4. Separate cords 1-4-1. Find the center 2 cords. Thread a size 6 frosted purple bead onto them, then tie a flat knot with cords 2 and 5.

5. We will now work with cords 1 and 6. With cord 1, thread on a seed bead, a dark purple size 6 bead and another seed bead. Repeat with cord 6, then separate the cords into 3-3. Tie a flat knot with the left 3 cords. Tie a flat knot with the right 3 cords.

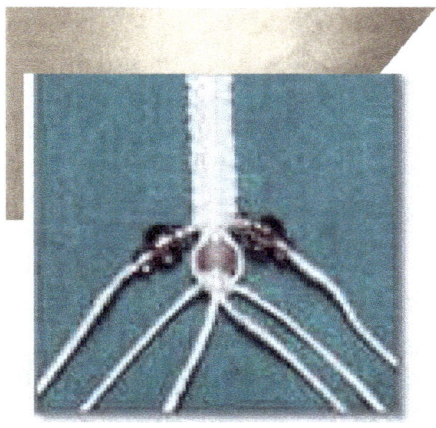 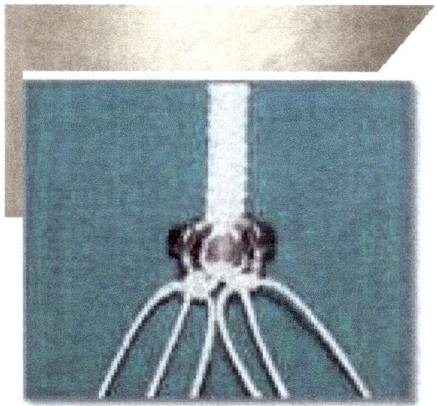

6. Repeat step 4 and 5 three times.

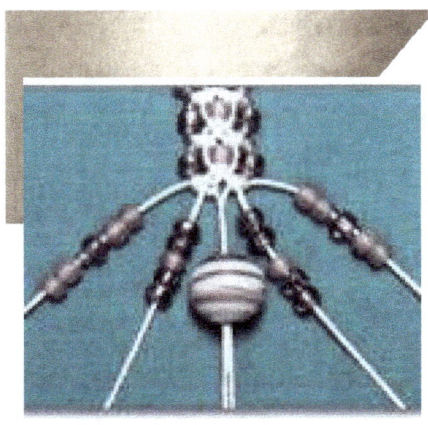

7. Find the center 2 cords, hold together and thread on the 1cm focal bead. Take the next cords out (2 and 5) and bead as follows: 2 size 6 dark purple beads, a frosted purple bead, 2 dark purple beads. Find cords 1 and 6 and bead as follows: 2 frosted purple beads, a seed bead, a dark purple bead, a seed bead, 2 frosted purple beads.

8. With cords 2 and 5, tie a flat knot around the center 2 cords. Place the center 4 cords together and tie a flat knot around them with outer cords 1 and 6.

9. Repeat steps 4 and 5 four times.

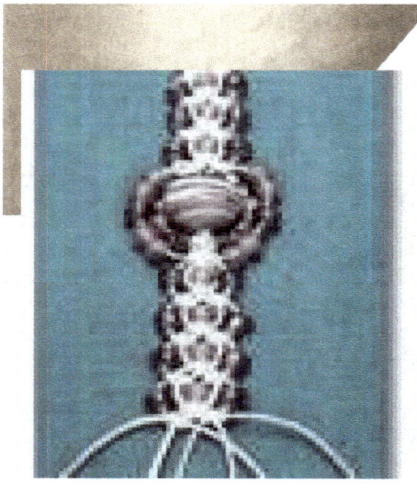

10. Repeat step 3.

11. Place your button bead on all 6 cords and tie an overhand knot tight against the bead. Glue well and trim the cords.

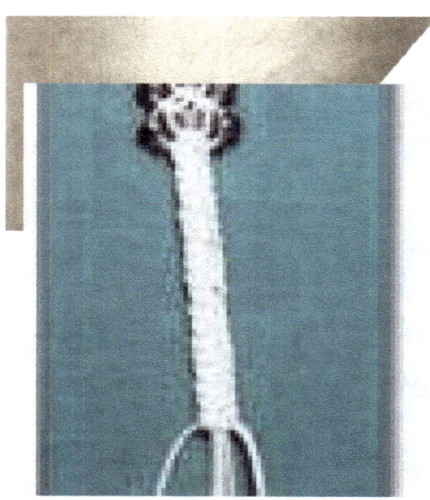
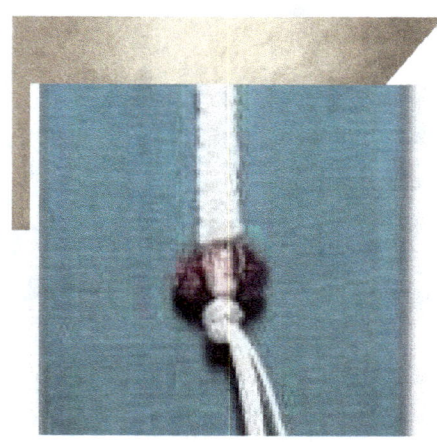

Project 13: Lantern Bracelet

This pattern may look simple, but please do not try it if you are in a hurry.

This one takes patience. Do not worry about getting your picot knots all in the exact same shape. Have fun with it! The finished bracelet is 7 ¼ inches in length. If desired, add a picot knot and a spiral knot on each side of the center piece to lengthen it. This pattern has a jump ring closure.

Knots Used:

- Lark's Head Knot
- Spiral Knot
- Picot Knot
- Overhand Knot

Supplies:

- 3 strands of C-Lon cord (2 light brown and 1 medium brown) 63-inch lengths
- Fasteners (1 jump ring, 1 spring ring or lobster clasp)

- Glue - Beacon 527 multi-use

- 8 small beads (about 4mm) amber to gold colors

- 30 gold seed beads

- 3 beads (about 6 mm) amber color (mine are rectangular, but round or oval will work wonderfully also)

- Note: Bead size can vary slightly. Just be sure all beads you choose will slide onto 2 cords (except seed beads).

Instructions:

1. Find the center of your cord and attach it to the jump ring with a lark's head knot. Repeat with the 2 remaining strands. If you want the 2-tone effect, be sure your second color is NOT placed in the center, or it will only be a filler cord and you will end up with a 1 tone bracelet.

2. You now have 6 cords to work with. Think of them as numbered 1 thorough 6, from left to right. Move cords 1 and 6 apart from

the rest. You will use these to work the spiral knot. All others are filler cords. Take cord number 1 tie a spiral knot. Always begin with the left cord. Tie 7 more spirals.

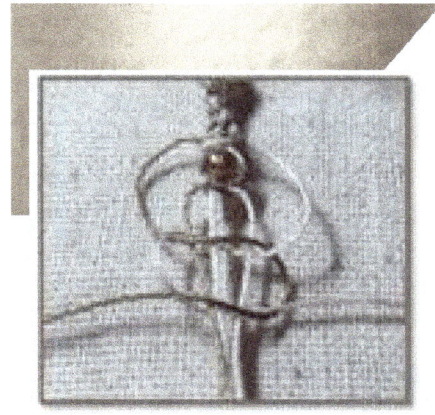

3. Place a 4mm bead on the center 2 cords. Leave cords 1 and 6 alone for now and work 1 flat knot using cords 2 and 5.

4. Now put cords 2 and 5 together with the center strands. Use 1 and 6 to tie a picot flat knot. If you do not like the look of your picot knot, loosen it up and try again. Gently tug the cords into place then lock in tightly with the next spiral knot.

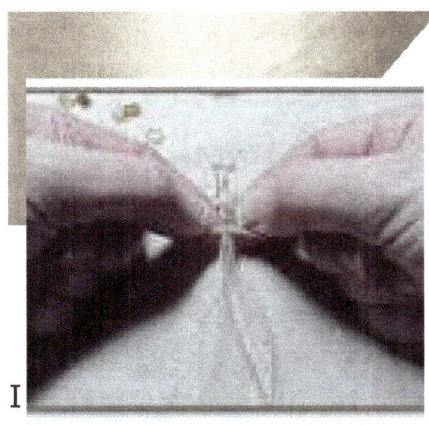

Notice here how I am holding the picot knot with my thumbs while pulling the cords tight with my fingers. If you look closely you may be able to see that I have a cord in each hand.

5. Tie 8 spiral knots (using left cord throughout pattern).

6. Place a 4mm bead on the center 2 cords. Leave cords 1 and 6 alone for now and work 1 flat knot using cords 2 and 5. Now put cords 2 and 5 together with the center strands. Use strands 1 and 6 to tie a picot flat knot.

7. Repeat steps 5 and 6 until you have 5 sets of spirals.

8. Next place 5 seed beads on cords 1 and 6. Put cords 3 and 4 together and string on a 6 mm bead. Tie one flat knot with the outermost cords.

Repeat this step two more times.

Now repeat steps 5 and 6 until you have 5 sets of spirals from the center point. Place a thread on your clasp. Tie an overhand knot with each cord and glue well. Let dry completely. As this is the weakest point in the design, advise trimming the excess cords and gluing again. Let dry.

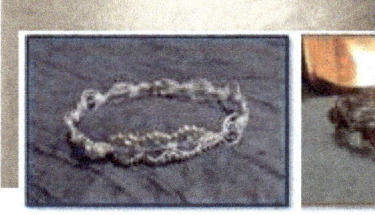

Project 14: Celtic Choker

Elegant loops allow the emerald and silver beads to stand out, making this a striking piece. The finished length is 12 inches. Be sure to use the ribbon clasp, which gives multiple length options to the closure.

Knots Used:

- Lark's Head Knot
- Alternating Lark's Head Chain

Supplies:

- 3 strands of black C-Lon cord; two 7ft cords, one 4ft cord
- 18 - green beads (4mm)
- 7 - round silver beads (10 mm)
- Fasteners: Ribbon Clasps, silver
- Glue - Beacon 527 multi-use

Note: Bead size can vary slightly. Just be sure all beads you choose will slide onto 2 cords.

Instructions:

1. Optional – Find the center of your cord and attach it to the top of the ribbon clasp with a lark's head knot. I found it easier to thread the loose ends through and pull them down until my loop was near the opening, then push the cords through the loop. Repeat with the 2 remaining strands, putting the four-foot cord in the center. If this is problematic, you could cut all the cords to 7ft and not worry about placement. (If you really trust your glue, you can skip this step by gluing the cords into the clasp and going from there).

2. Lay all cords into the ribbon clasp. Add a generous dap of glue and use pliers to close the clasp.

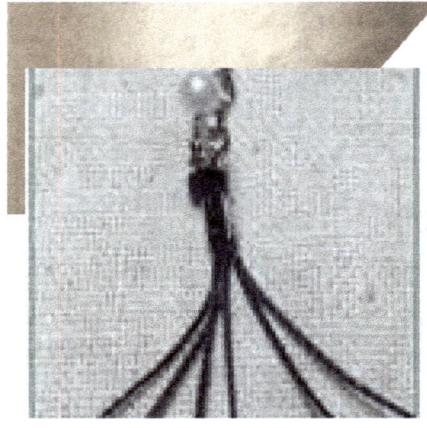

3. You now have 6 cords to work with. Find the 4 ft cords and place them in the center. They will be the holding (or filler) cords throughout.

4. Begin your Alternating Lark's Head (ALH) chain, using the outmost right cord then the outermost left cord. Follow with the other right cord then the last left cord. For this first set, the pattern will be hard to see. You may need to tug gently on the cords to get a little slack in them.

5. Now slide a silver bead onto the center 2 cords.

 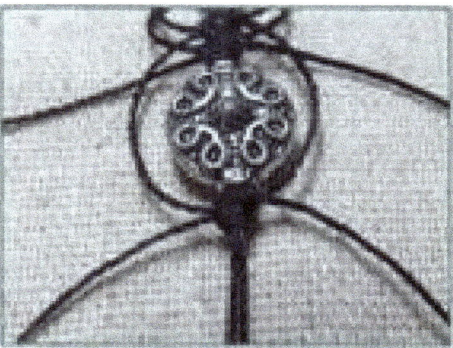

6. The outer cords are now staggered on your holding cords. Continue with the ALH chain by knotting with the upper right cord... then tie a knot with the upper left cord.

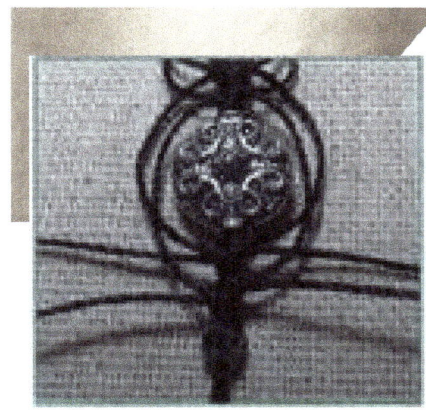

7. Finish your set of 4 knots, then add a green bead

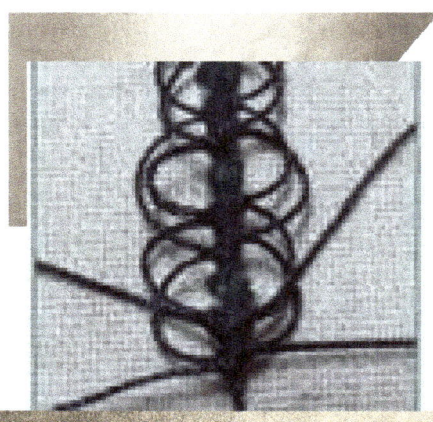

8. Tie four ALH knots followed by a green bead until you have 3 green beads in the pattern. Then tie one more set of 4 ALH knots.

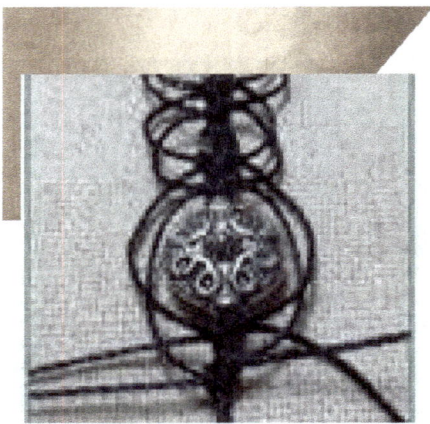

9. Slide on a silver bead and continue creating sequences of 3 green, 1 silver (always with 4 ALH knots between each). End with the 7th silver bead and 1 more set of 4 ALH knots, for a 12" necklace.

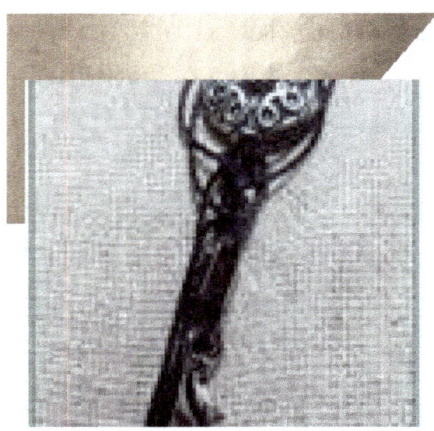

10. Lay all cords in the ribbon clasp and glue well.

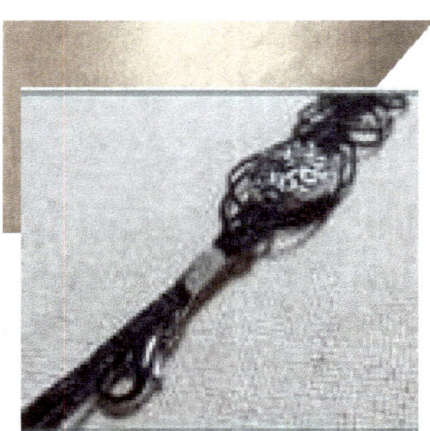

11. Crimp shut and let dry completely. Trim excess cords.

CHAPTER - 7
MACRAMÉ BRACELET IV

Project 15: Climbing Vine Keychain

This pattern is a fun way to practice the Diagonal Double Half-Hitch knot. It works up quickly and is a fun piece to work in various colors. Just be sure to use enough beads on the fringe work to weigh the threads down.

- Knots Used:
- Lark's Head
- Flat Knot
- Diagonal Double Half-Hitch

Supplies:

- Measure out 3 cords of Peridot C-Lon, 30" each

- 1 key ring
- 2 (5mm) beads
- 8 (plus extra for ends) pink seed beads
- 4 (plus extra for ends) gold seed beads
- 12 (plus extra for ends) green seed beads
- 8 (plus extra for ends) 3mm pearl beads (seed pearl beads will work also)
- Glue - Beacon 527 multi-use

Note: You can vary slightly the bead size. Just be sure that 2 cords will fit through the 2 main beads (the 5mm size beads).

Instructions:

1. Fold each cord in half and use a lark's head knot to attach it to the key ring. Secure onto your work surface with straight pins. You now have 6 cords to work with.

MACRAMÉ PROJECTS

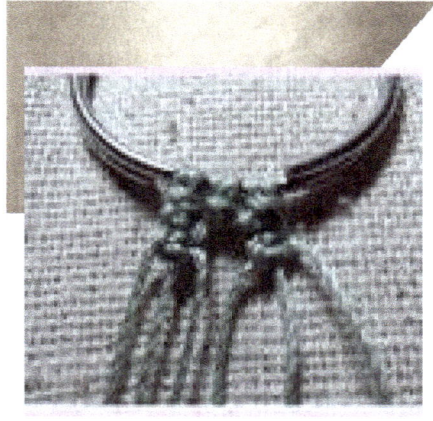

2. Separate cords into 3 and 3. Using the left 3 cords, tie 2 flat knots. Repeat with the right 3 cords.

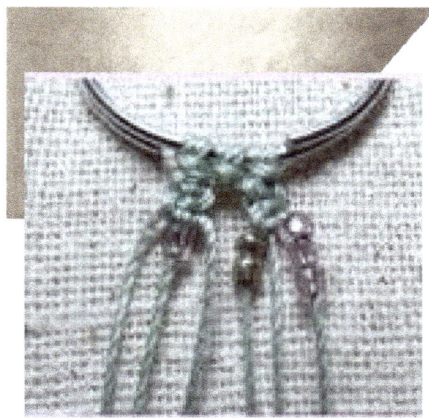

3. Place all six cords together and think of them as numbered 1-6, left to right. Skip cord 1 and place a pink seed bead on cord 2. Skip cord 3 and place 2 gold seed beads on cord 4. Skip cord 5 and put 3 pink seed beads on cord 6.

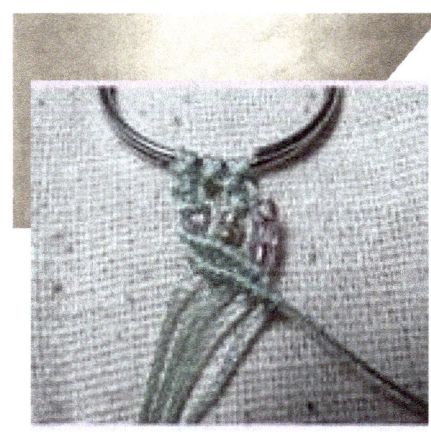

4. Using cord 1 as your holding cord, tie a row of diagonal double half-hitch (DDHH) knots beginning on the left and ending on the right. Using cord 1 on the left, move it to the right as a holding cord and tie

DDHH knots to the right.

5. Put all six cords together. Place 7 small beads on cord 1. Skip cord 2 and string your focal bead onto cords 3 and 4. Skip cord 5 and put 3 small beads on cord 6.

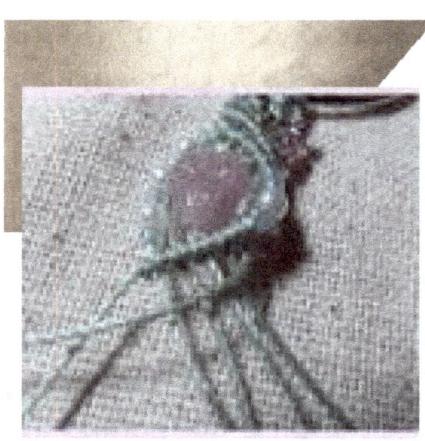

6. Use cord 6 as your holding cord and tie a row of DDHH knots from right to left. Repeat once more.

7. Repeat beading from step 3.

8. Repeat a row of diagonal double half-hitch knots from step 4 (left to right) twice.

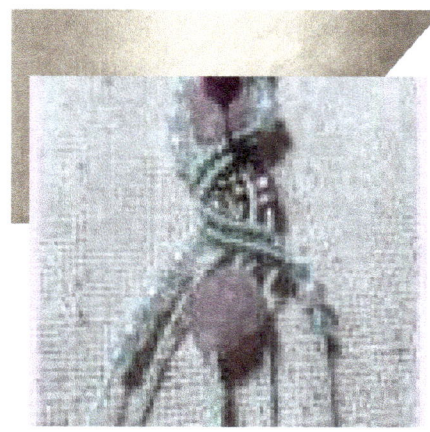

9. Place a bead as stated in step 5.

10. Repeat a row of DDHH knots as written in step 6 (right to left) twice.

11. Separate cords into 3 and 3. Tie 1 flat knot with the left 3 cords and 2 flat knots with the right 3 cords.

12. Separate cords into 1 – 4 – 1 and tie 1 flat knot with the center 4 cords only, letting cords 1 and 6 float.

13. Separate cords into 3 and 3. Tie 1 flat knot with each section.

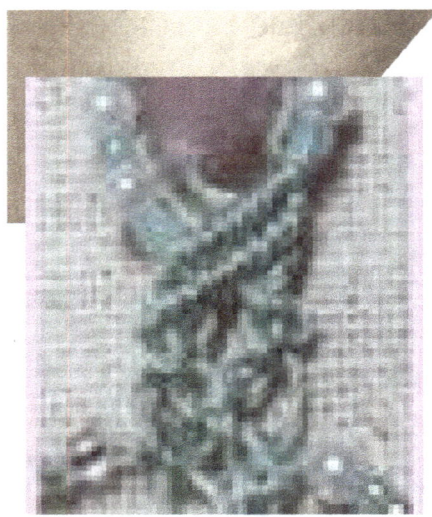

14. Repeat step 12.

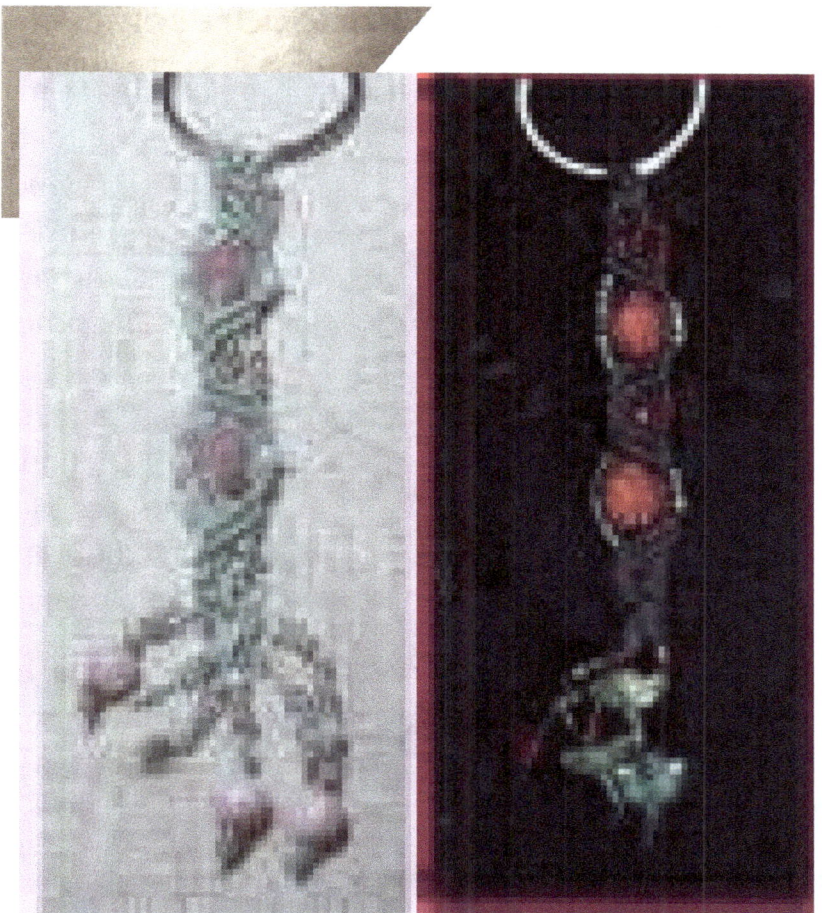

15. Bead ends with various size beads. Be sure there is enough weight to hold the ends downward. Tie an overhand knot with each cord and glue well. Let dry completely and trim cords.

Project 16: Filigree Lacelet Bracelet

Let us put it all together. This last project uses many of the knots learned in the previous compositions. The Overhand knot, Flat knot, Alternating Lark's Head knot and Diagonal Double Half Hitch knot are all in play here.

This "Lace-let" fits the very definition of filigree as it is both delicate and fanciful. I hope you enjoy this design that is open and light. The finished length is 7 1/2 inches and includes a button closure.

Knots Used:

- Overhand Knot
- Diagonal Double Half Hitch
- Flat Knot
- Alternating Lark's Head Knot

Supplies:

- 66" length white C-Lon cord, 4 strands
- 6 clear beads, 5mm

- 56 clear beads, 3mm
- 5 clear beads, 4mm
- 1 bead for button closure, about 7mm
- 164 clear seed beads
- Glue - Beacon 527 multi-use

Note: You can vary the bead sizes slightly. Just be sure the beads you choose will slide onto 2, and sometimes 3 cords. (The seed beads only need to fit onto one cord).

Instructions:

1. Find the center of the cords and lightly tie an overhand knot. Pin this onto your project board. Tie about 9 flat knots (for 7mm button closure bead). Now undo the overhand knot and fold the flat knots into a horseshoe shape. Using the outer cord from each side, tie 1 flat knot.

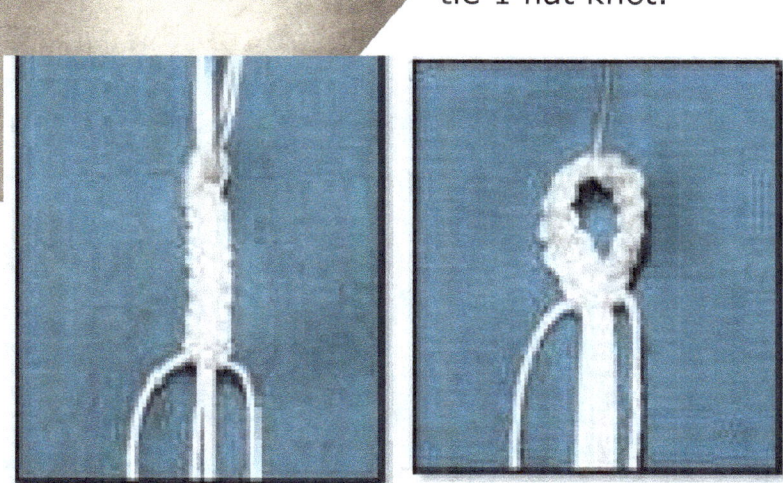

2. Take the rightmost cord and place it over all others down to the left to work Diagonal Double Half Hitch (DDHH) knots from right to left. Put 1 clear seed bead on each cord, then tie another set of DDHH knots from right to left.

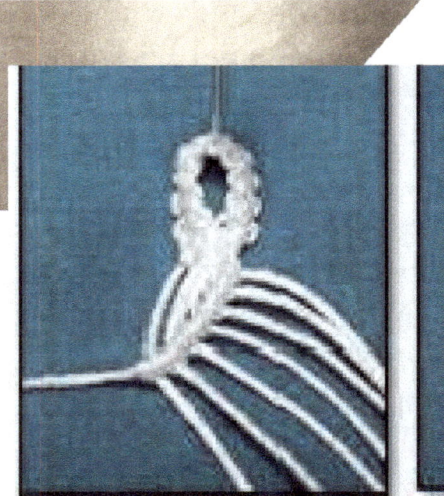
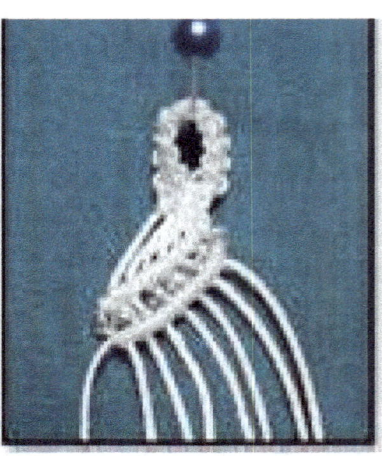

3. Separate cords into 4-4. Working with left 4 cords bead as follows: on the left most, cord put 4 clear 3mm beads with a seed bead between each one. The next cord in gets 5 clear seed beads. The next cord in needs a 5mm clear bead. And the last cord of this section gets 5 clear seed beads. Use the outer 2 cords to tie a flat knot around the inner cords.

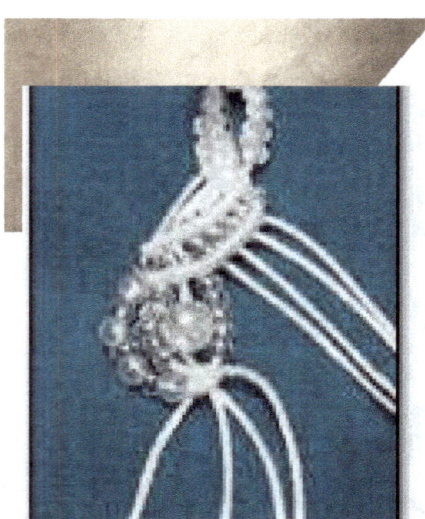

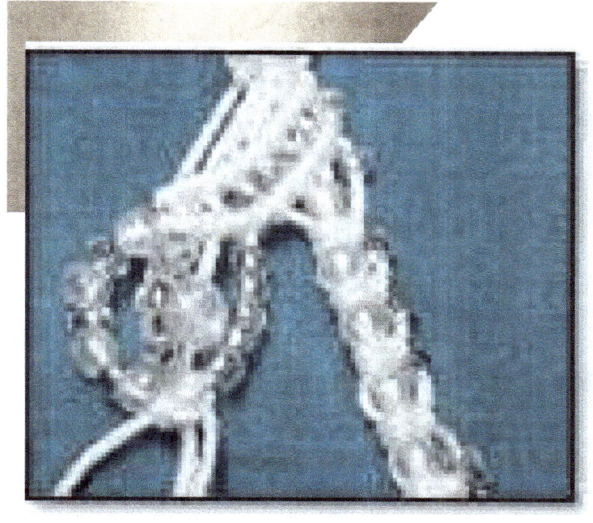

4. Working with right 4 cords: Place a 3mm clear bead on the center 2 cords. Place a seed bead on the right most cord. Now use this right most cord to tie an Alternating Lark's Head (ALH) knot around the other 3 cords. Repeat 4 times.

5. Using the left most cord as a holding cord, work DDHH knots from left to right. Place a seed bead on each cord then work another set of DDHH knots (from left to right again) using the left most cord as your holding cord.

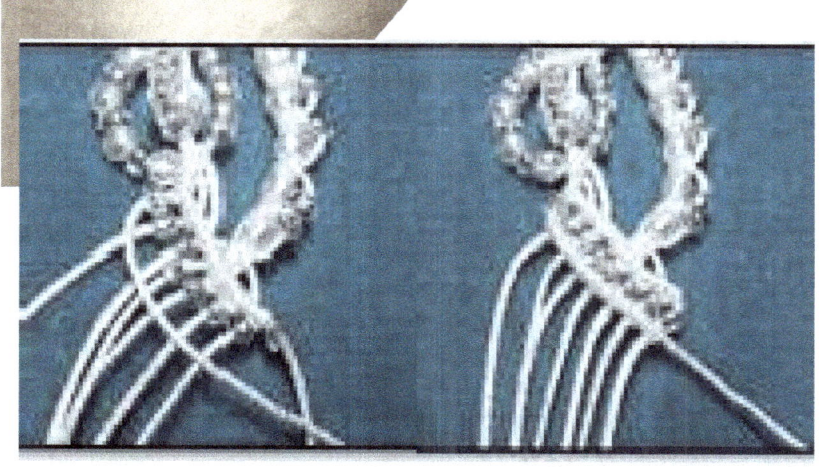

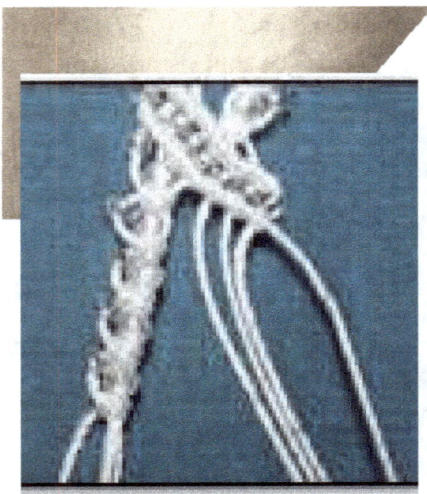

6. Separate cords into 4-4. Working with left 4 cords: Place a 3mm clear bead on the center 2 cords. Place a seed bead on the left most cord. Now use this left most cord to tie an ALH knot around the other 3 cords. Repeat 4 times.

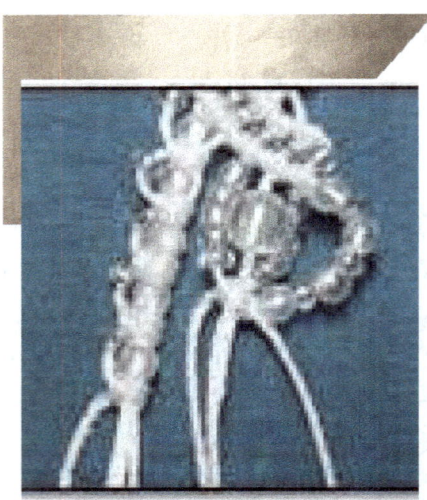

7. Working with right 4 cords: the right most cord gets 4 clear 3mm beads with a seed bead between each one. The next cord in from the right needs 5 seed beads. The next cord in gets a 5mm clear bead. And the last cord of this section gets 5 seed beads. Use the outer 2 cords to tie a flat knot around the inner cords.

8. Repeat steps 2-7 for pattern until you have about 6 1/2 inches in length.

9. Separate cords into 3-2-3. On the left set of cords, place a 4mm bead. With the center 2 cords thread on a 3mm bead, a 4mm bead and another 3mm bead. On the right 3 cords place three 4mm beads. Find the outermost cord on each side and tie a flat knot around the rest.

10. Thread your button bead onto the center 4, or 6 cords if possible. Use the outer cords to tie a flat knot. Glue flat knot and let dry. Trim excess cords.

CHAPTER - 8
MACRAMÉ PATTERN: FASHION ITEM

Project 17: Striped Clutch Handbags

This Clutch showcases picots with the sides of flap. A symmetrical stripe is created by using a 2nd color and switching between the right and left Square Knots. It is an extremely easy Macramé project, appropriate for a beginner. You must have some practice of tying Square Knots both left and right, but they are all explained as portion of the instructions. The dimensions of the finished clutch purse are 6.5 inches height (folded) and 9 inches wide. You can effortlessly create a broader version by adding more strings to it. Like the example illustrated, we are using two colors. A color is a brown, and B color is turquoise; you can use any color according to your preference.

Materials Needed:

- 50 yards) 4mm string material
- A small size button for the clasp

- Project board, some pins, glue, and tape

Knots Used:

- Barrel Knot (BK)
- Double Half Hitch (DHH)
- Alternating Square Knots (ASK)
- Square Knot (right and left both)

Preparation:

- Cut twenty cords of color A, each 4 yards in length.

- Cut extra strings into sets of two to keep the Clutch (striped) larger than 9 inches, make sure you have an even number of strands.

- Cut four cords of color B, each 4 yards in length.

Step by Step Instructions:

1. Fold in half two of A color cords and tie them in the middle. The following picture shows you how to wrap a (Left Square) Knot at the flap edge to form the picots. You can use these same set of details to produce all the left Square Knot used in creating the body of your Striped Clutch. Mentally mark the four parts, like they were four separate strings. For the left Square Knot, you always start by moving strand 1 towards the right, over filler cords 2 to 3 and under your working strand 4.

Now move 4 cord to the left, under filler cords 2 to 3,

and over the working string 1.

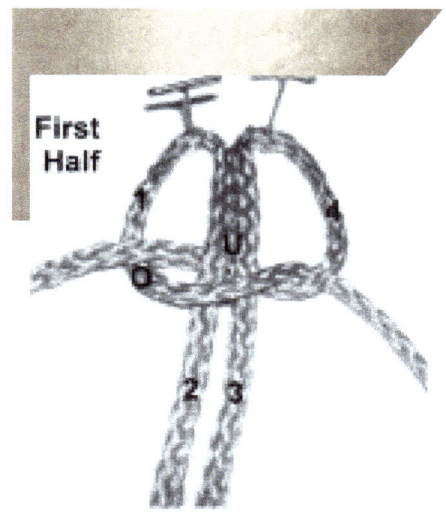

Shift the knot's first half so that it sits half-inch below the fold (for half-inch picot). Cords 4 and 1 have changed places, and the position for the 2nd half of the SK is now reversed.

Pull cord 1 towards the left, over strings 2 to 3, and underneath cord 4. Pull cord 4 towards the right, underneath cords 2 - 3, and over cord 1.

2. Revise 1 step with two cords in color B, making 1 picot loop design.

3. The following guidelines are for the right Knot (SK) picot designs. Create at least seven picots with A color design. If you want the clutch that is striped to be broader than nine inches, you can make more picots in this color.

4. Create one picot with B color at the top.

For your right Square know, you begin by pulling 4 cord towards the left, over strings 2 to 3 and underneath strand 1. Now move strand 1 to the right, underneath strands 2 to 3, and over your working cord 4.

Move cord 4 to the right for the second half, over the filler cords 2-3 and underneath cord 1. Pull cord 1 towards the left, underneath cord 2-3, and over 4 cord.

5. Organize on the board all picot designs as follows: Three A colors Left picots (from steps 1 to 2), followed by one B color Left picot design created in step 3. And one B color right picot created in step 4 that is follow by the 7 color A picot designs.

Any other picot designs that you have created needs

to be placed on the right side of others.

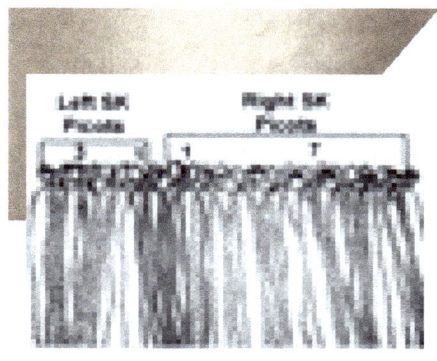

The Clutch that is striped is created using (ASK) Alternating Square Knots. Before beginning, you must know how to switch cords, so if you do not know about how pattern of ASK work, then practice. For each row, you will begin from the left, so the directions make sense. Mentally number all the cords from 1 - 48. Pay very clear focus on the direction of your Square Knot (left or right), as the stripe made with B color depends on the changes in direction. Left SK: The working cords on the left-hand side is moved first. Right SK: First, working cords moved will be on the right.

6. The 1st row is tied in groups of 4, starting with cord 3.

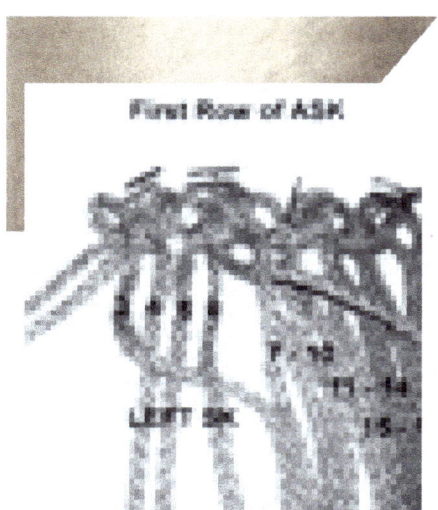

The first 4 knots are left Square Knot made with the cords:

- 3 - 6 of color A
- 7 - 10 of color A
- 11 – 14 of color B and A combined
- 15 - 18 of color B

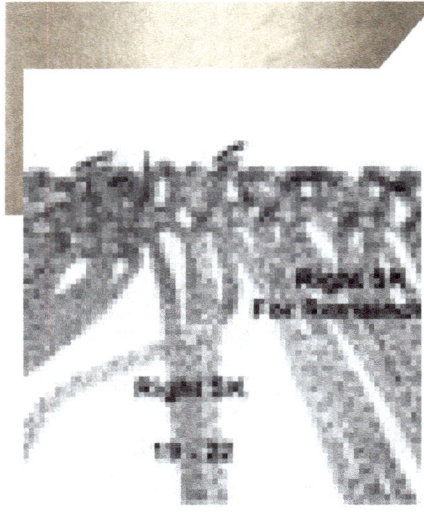

7. Now change to a right Square Knot when for which you are using cords 19 to 22, which is of the knots remaining cords used are 27 - 43 – 46 color B and A combined. are all right Square Knots, of A color: 30, 23 26, 35 38, 31 34 and 39 42.

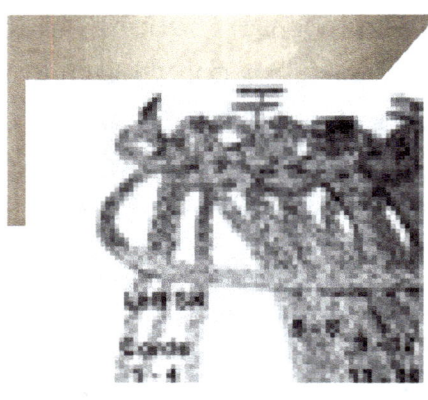

8. The 2nd of the row starts with the 4 remaining SK, tied with cords: o 1 - 4 (A color)

- 5 - 8 (A color)
- 9 - 12 (A color)
- 13 - 16 (B color)

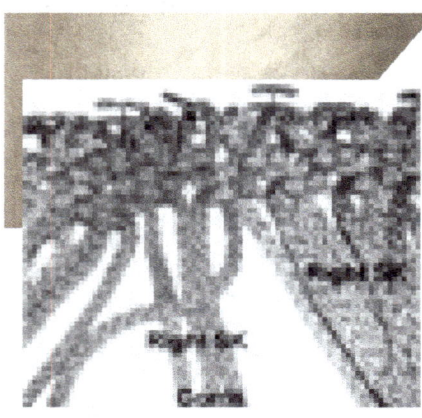

9. Tie the 1st right square knot with cords 17 to 20, of color B.

The leftover loops are tied with the cords:

- 21 to 24,
- 25 to 28,

- 29, 32,
- 33 to 36,
- 37 to 40,
- 41 to 44 and
- 45 to 48.

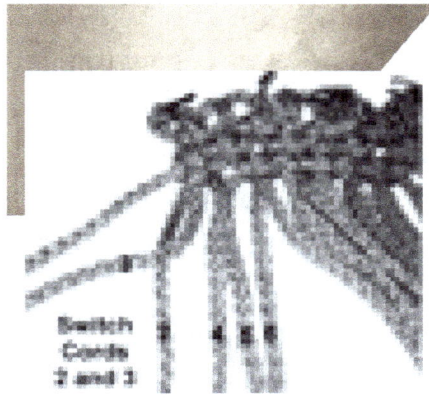

10. Redo 6th step but switch cords 2 & 3 before you do so. So, the first left Square Knot is created with cords 2-4-5-6. Cord 2 is required to be used as a cord working only one time, and this is good spot to do it.

Repeat 7th step but switch cords 47 and 46 when you reach to the last ASK of that row. Now cords 43-44-45, and 47 will tie the final right Square Knot.

11. You repeat the steps 9 and 8 and then steps 7 and 6 for the rest of the striped clutch.

12. Repeat this step until the pattern is eighteen inches in length, from the top to the end row of ASK

of the picots. Stop on the row where cords 3 to 46 are used (steps 7 and 6).

Useful tip: Notice to make sure that the cords of color B are in the group always before starting each row. It is

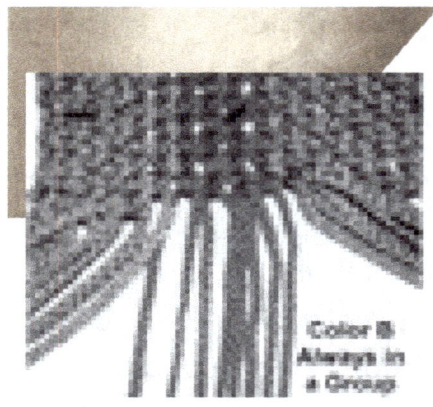

effortless to change cords around unintentionally, and That is BAD in this case. So be very careful while you are in the area that is striped and pay clear attention towards the cord position (see the picture for reference).

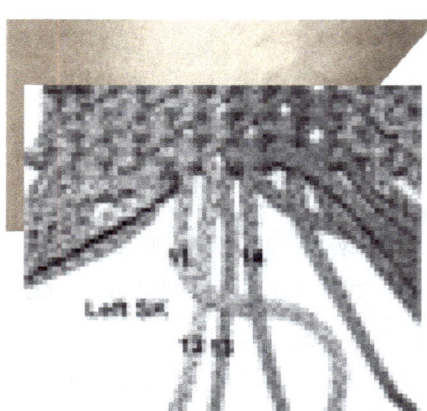

The two colors are blended on a stripe in the rows where the steps repeat 7 and 6. The Square knot is always started with the color A thread. For this situation, that is chord 11 since you are tying a left Square Knot.

In this row, the next blended color knot also begins with the same working cord of color A.

That is string 22 in this situation since you are creating a right Square Knot.

The last detail that you should observe is that the first

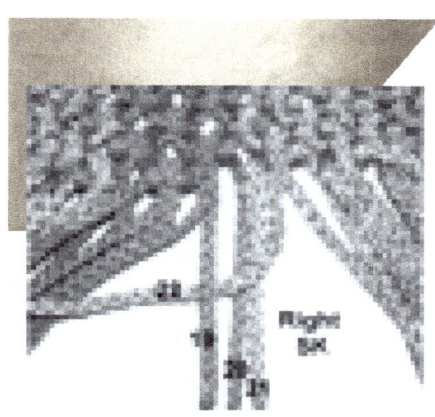

4 knots are all left Square Knots in each row, and the remainder are right SK's. Again, rightly changing directions at the right place is very important for creating this Striped Clutch. The lines will not be aligned otherwise.

The Striped Clutch's front edge is made once all the ASK is attached or tied. Ensure that you have complete idea to tie a (DHH) Double Half Hitches.

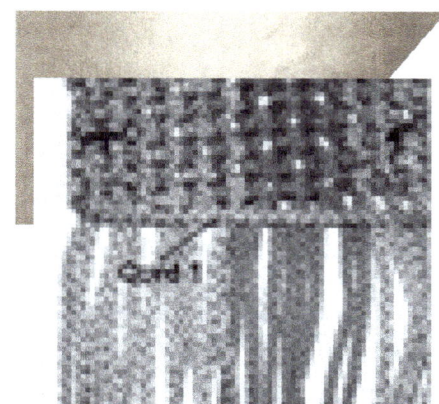

13. Pull 1 cord to the right, and so it lies on above of all other string.

14. This cord will work as a holding or stopping cord for the first row of DHH's.

15. Connect cords 2 to 47 with DHH knot to holding 1 cord. While creating each loop, rotating counterclockwise. Securely tie each knot.

The formed bar should be placed against the last ASK row and bent a little to the right and left edges of the purse (just like in the next picture).

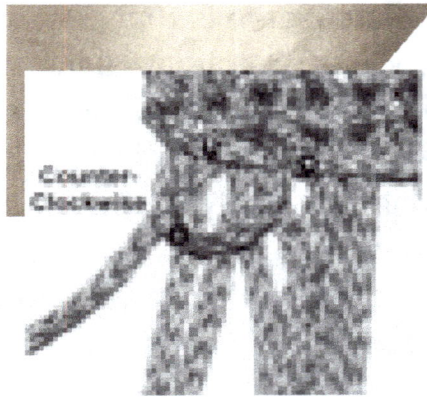

When you move forwards, push the ties as tight as you can to one another, so that you have space for all the cords. Make sure that you do not connect cord 48 that is the last cord from the edge that is right to your Striped Clutch.

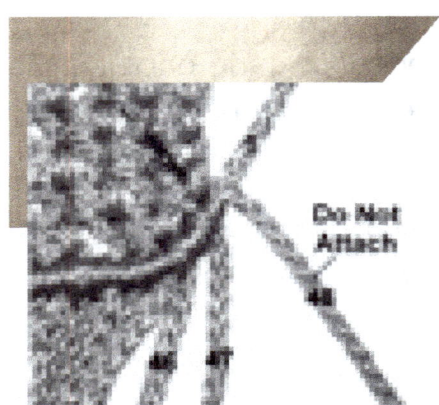

16. Now move cord 48 towards the left, located just below DHH's first section. Connect all the cords 47 to 2 in the same order with clockwise DHH knots. Once you got to the striped area, stop there.

17. End the strings by cutting them down to two inches each. Flip the clutch that is striped, so you are now working with the back. Slide single cord through the loop created under 1 row, which is the row underneath the ASK row. Use tweezers and pliers if needed for this step. This clutch must be lined, hiding the cut corners of the cords. If you do not want to do this, cut the cords a bit more, and add glue to stick them to the inside layer. You should burn (heat) the tips with a fire if using synthetic materials like nylon, to melt the substance at the edges to avoid the fray.

MACRAMÉ PROJECTS

18. Now it is safe to lace the slides up to the clutch. Begin by taking measurement of the clutch down to five inches, starting from the picots. That is the flap of your clutch, so fold it here. Pull down 6 and half inches and again fold it. This will separate the back to the front end. The section with the DHH knots is your front. Grip the bag between your thighs or place it on one corner. There are knots in between the rows of Alternating Square Knot along the sides of the clutch. Line up the knots at the back and front sections so they are in direct to each other. There will be a single knot at the fold in the front and the back. Use two 18 "scrap cord pieces, or two new pieces, to tie the edges.

Slip your lacing cord in the end rows of DHH's make sure you are as near to the edge as feasible from the

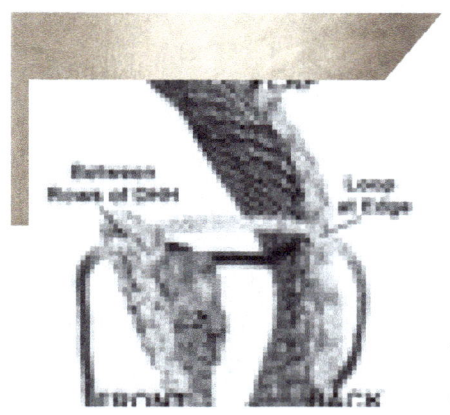

front of the clutch. Now slide it straight across a loop from the back of the clutch.

19. Make a cross using the two ends of your lacing cord's, and then move them into the loops of next set. Move them from in to outside.

20. Redo 18th step several times more, bypassing the ends from another loops, till you meet the flipped (folded) area in the front and the back. Once you reach the fold, move both your ends from the similar loop, bringing them to the inner side of your Striped Clutch.

Before you go on, ensure the lacing is firm.

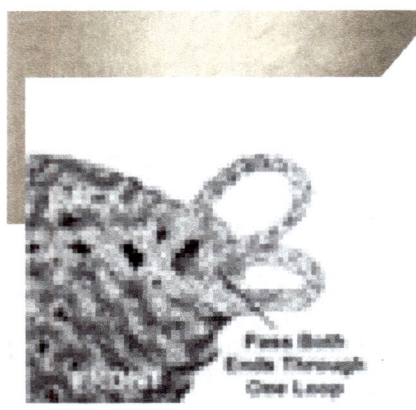

21. Turn the clutch inside out, so that the lacing string is on the outer side and easier to handle. Hold a Barrel Knot (Extra Loop and Overhand Knot) to hold it in place. Trim off the excess material near the knot, then add a little glue to it. When you are using a synthetic material cord, you can melt the material with the fire. Flip the clutch that is striped inside out, so that the edges that are cut are on the inner side.

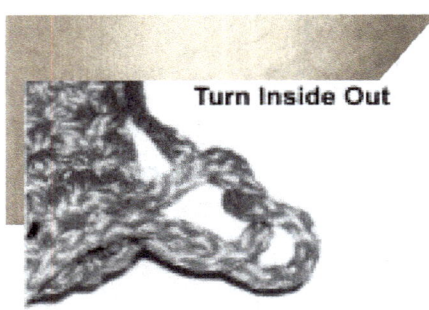

22. You can add a lining into it right around the ends. The good area to stitch it in the forward area is inside the (two) rows of DHH. There is enough area for a thread and needle.

CHAPTER - 9
PLANT HANGERS

Project 18: Plant Hanger Ayla

Description: Plant hanger of 2 feet and 3,5 inches (70 cm)

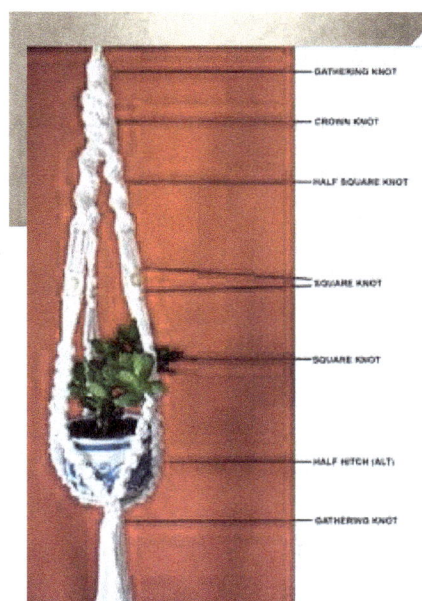

Used Knots:

- Square knot,
- Half square knot,
- Alternating square knot,
- Crown knot,
- Gathering knot and half hitch knot

Supplies:

- 4 strands of cord of 13 feet and 1,5 inches (4 meter),
- 4 strands of 16 feet and 4,8 inches (5 meter),
- 2 strands of 3 feet and 3,4 inches (1 meter),
- 1 wooden ring of 2 inches (50 mm) and

- 4 wooden beads: diameter 0,4 inches (10mm)

Directions (step-by-step):

1. Fold the 8 longer strands of cord in half through the wooden ring. Tie all (now 16) strands together with 1 shorter strand of 3 feet and 3,4 inches (1 m) with a gathering knot. Cut the cord ends off after tying the gathering knot.

2. Now follows the crown knot. It is the easiest when you turn your project up-side-down in between your legs, as shown on the photos. Divide the 16 strands into 4 sets of 4 strands each. Each set has 2 long strands and 2 shorter strands. Tie 5 crown knots in each set. Pull each strand tight and smooth.

3. Tie 15 half square knots on each set of four strands. In each set the 2 shorter strands are in the middle and you are tying with the 2 outer, longer strands. Drop down 2,4 inches (6 cm of no knots).

4. Tie 1 square knot with each set.

5. Then add the wooden bead to the 2 inner cords of each set and tie 1 square knot with each set again. Drop down 2,4 inches (6 cm of no knots) and tie 6 square knots with each of the 4 sets.

6. Take 2 strands of 1 set and make 10 alternating half hitch knots. Repeat for the 2 left strands of that set. And then repeat for all sets.

7. Tie an alternating square knot to connect the left two cords in each set with the right two of the set next to it. Followed by 3 square knots for each new set (so you have 4 square knots in total for each new formed set).

8. Place your chosen container/bowl into the hanger to make sure it will fit, gather all strands together and then tie a gathering knot with the left-

over shorter strand of 3 feet and 3,4 inches (1 m). Trim all strands to the length that you want. If you want, you can unravel the ends of each strand.

Project 19: Plant Hanger Bella

Description: Plant hanger of 60 cm (not counting the fringe)

Supplies:

- 6 strands of cord of 13 feet and 1,5 inches (4 meter),
- 4 strands of 16 feet and 4,8 inches (5 meter) and
- A wooden stick of 11,8 inches (30cm)

Used Knots:

- Half knot,
- Lark´s Head knot,
- Square knot (Alternating) and Coil knot

Directions (step-by-step):

1. Fold all strands in half and tie them to the wooden stick with Lark´s Head knot. The longest strands are on the outer side (2 strands at the left side and 2 at the right).

2. Make 4 rows of alternating square knots. (See knot guide for explanation)

3. In the 5th row you only make 2 alternating square knots on the right and 2 on the left.

4. In the 6th row you only tie 1 alternating square on each side.

5. Then, with the 4 strands on the side, you tie 25 half (square) knots. Do this for both sides, left and right side.

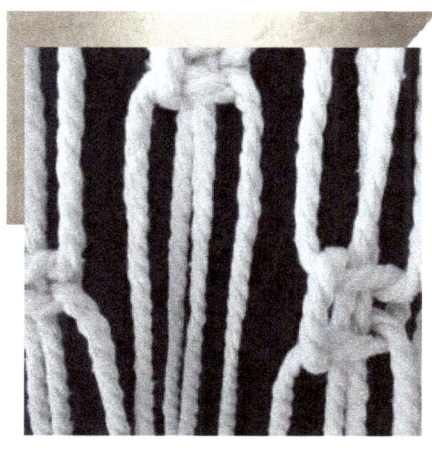

6. Take 4 strands from the middle of the plant hanger, first drop down 2,4 inches (6 cm of no knots) and then tie a square knot with the 4 center strands. Now with the 4 strands next to the middle, drop down 3,15 inches (8 cm of no knots), and tie a square knot. Do this for both sides (left and right).

7. Drop down 2,4 inches (6 cm of no knots) and tie 2 (alternated) square knots by taking 2 strands from both sides (right and left group). Then 3 alternating square knots with the other groups. These knots must be about at the same height where the strands with the half knots have ended.

8. Take the 2 outer strands of the left group, which you made 25 half knots, and take the 2 outer strands of the group on the right. First dropping down 2,4 inches (6 cm of no knots), you tie a square knot with these 4 strands.

9. Do the same with the rest of the strands left over, make groups of 4 strands, and tie alternated square knots on the same height as the one you made

in step 8. Drop down 2,4 inches (6 cm of no knots) and make another row of alternated square knots using all strands.

10. Drop down 2,4 inches (6 cm of no knots) and make 5 rows of alternated square knots. Be careful: this time leave NO space in between the alternated square knots and you make them as tight as possible.

11. Drop down as many inches/cm as you want to make the fringe and tie at all ends a coil knot.

12. Then cutoff all strands, directly under each coil knot.

Project 20: Plant Hanger Cathy

Description: Plant hanger of 2 feet and 9,5 inches (85 cm) - not counting the fringe

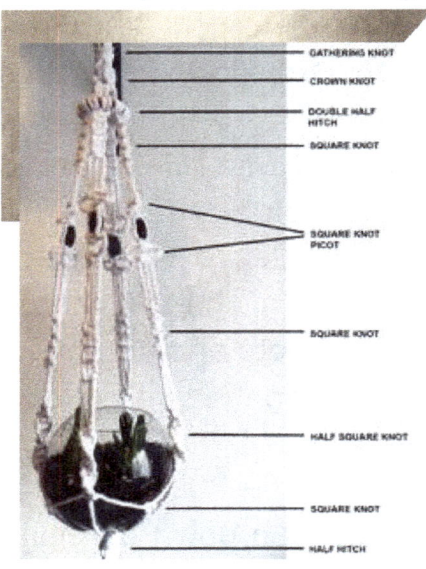

Supplies:

- 4 wooden beads of 1,2 inches (3cm),
- 3 inches (7,5cm) wooden ring,
- 4 cords of 18 feet (5,5 meter),
- 2 cords of 15 feet (4,5 meter) and
- 1 cord of 2 feet and 1,6 inches (65 centimeters)

Used Knots:

- Gathering knot,
- Crown knot, (double) half hitch,
- Half square knot and Square knot

Directions (step-by-step):

1. Fold the 6 longer cords in half, placing the loops neatly side by side. Use a gathering knot for tying the cords together with the shortest cord. This gives you twelve cords in total.

MACRAMÉ PROJECTS

2. Arrange the cords in four groups of three cords each. Make sure that each group consist out of 2 longer cords and 1 shorter cord. Tie three Chinese Crown knots with the four groups of cords.

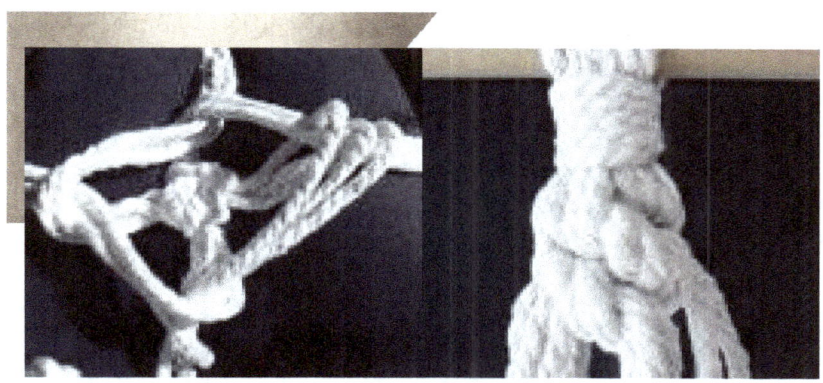

3. Slip the wooden ring over the top loop and drop it down 1,2 inches (3 cm) from the last Chinese Crown knot. With each of the twelve cords, tie one double half hitch on the ring to secure it. This gives you a ring of double half hitches.

4. Arrange the cords into four groups of three cords each. The middle cord of each group is the shorter one, this is called the filler cord. Repeat step five thru eight for each group.

5. Tie four square knots, each having one shorter, filler cord.

6. Skip down 2 inches (5 cm). Tie one square knot picot.

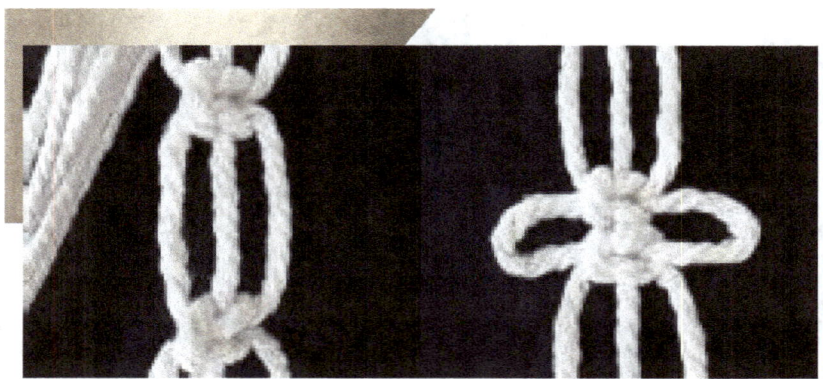

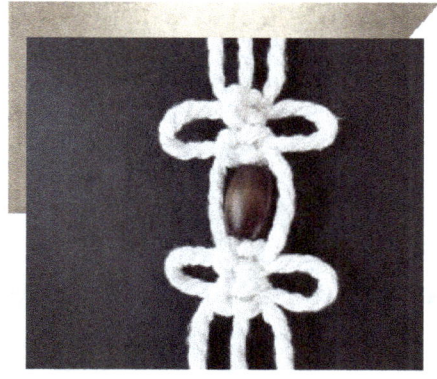

7. Slide a bead up the filler cord. Tie another square knot picot directly under the bead.

8. Skip down 2 inches (5 cm). Tie five square knots, each having one filler cord.

9. Skip down 2 inches (5 cm). Tie 10 half square knots, each having one filler cord.

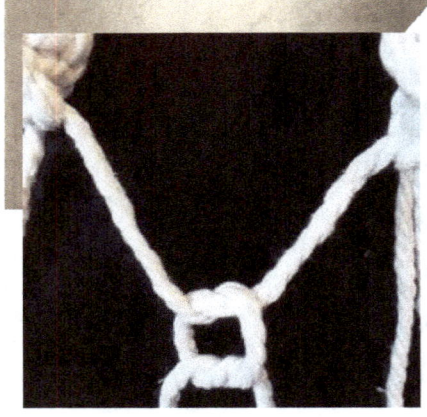

10. Repeat the following procedure for each of the four groups you have just knotted: skip down 2,4 inches (6 cm); take one cord from each neighboring square knot to tie a square knot WITHOUT a filler cord. This gives you four square knots made of two cords each. The cords in the middle of each group are NOT used to knot.

11. Skip down 4,8 inches (12 cm). Gather and tie all cords together with one of cords hanging using to tie 10 times a half hitch.

12. Cut the fringe to measure 6 inches (15 cm).

CHAPTER - 10
Backdrop, Wall Arts, Home Decors

Macramé Home Décor

Now, it is time to learn how to make various home decors—simply by using the art of Macramé! Check them out and see which ones you want to make yourself!

Project 21: Modern Macramé Hanging Planter

Plant hangers are beautiful because they give your house or garden the feel of an airy, natural space. This one is perfect for condominiums or small apartments—and for those with minimalist, modern themes!

Plant Pot

Supplies:

> 50 ft. Par cord (Parachute Cord)
> 16 to 20 mm wooden beads

First, fold in half 4 strands of the cord and then loop so you could form a knot.

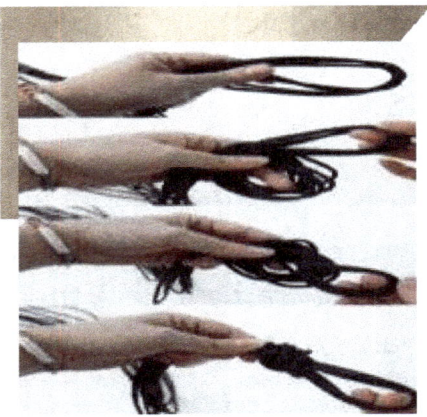

Now, divide the cords into groups of two and make sure to string 2 cords through one of the wooden beads you have on hand. String some more beads—at least 4 on each set of 2 grouped cords.

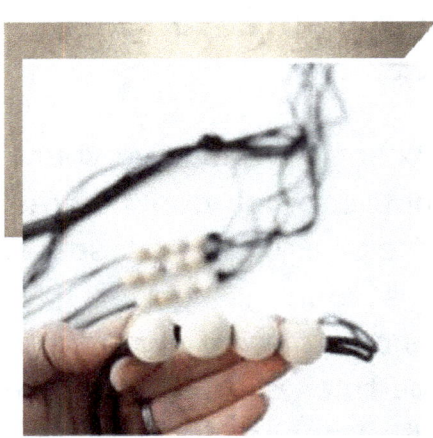

Then, measure every 27.5 inches and tie a knot at that point and repeat this process for every set of cords.

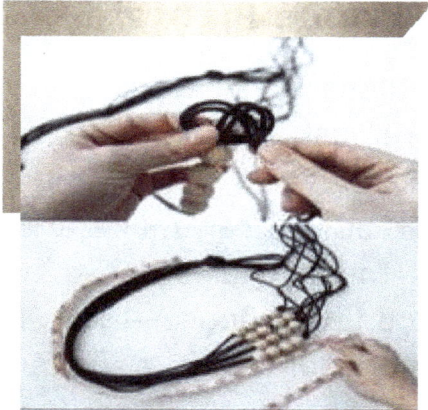

Look at the left set of the cord and tie it to the right string. Repeat on the four sets so that you could make at least 3" from the knot you have previously made.

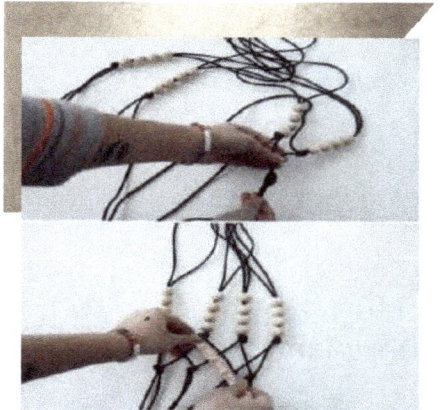

Tie another four knots from the previous knot that you have made. Make them at least 4.5" each.

Group all the cords together and tie a knot to finish the planter. You will get something like the one shown below—and you could just add your very own planter to it!

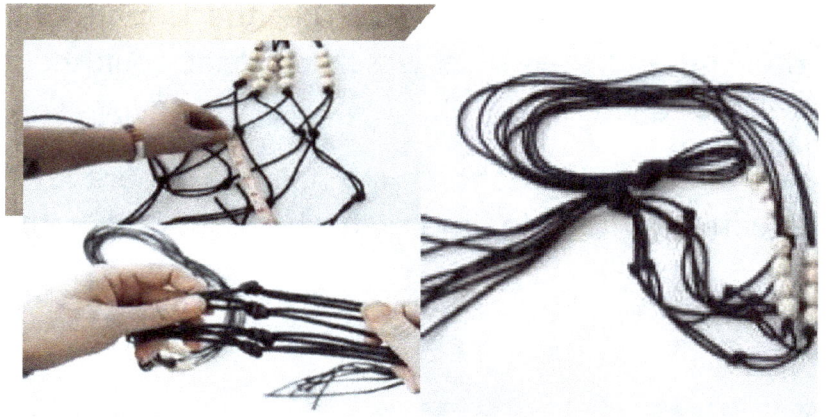

Project 22: Mini Macramé Planters

Succulents are all the rage these days because they are just so cute and are decorative! What is more is that you can make a lot of them and place them around the house—that will give your place a unique look!

Supplies:

- Small container
- Garden soil/potting mix
- Succulents/miniature plants
- ¼ inch jump ring
- 8 yards embroidery thread or thin cord

Cut 36-inch of 8 lengths of cord. Make sure that 18 inches are already enough to cover enough half-hitches. If not, you can always add more. Let the thread loop over the ring and then tie a wrap knot that could hold all the cords together.

Create a half-twist knot by tying half of a square knot and repeating it multiple times with the rest of the cord.

Drop a quarter inch of the cord down and repeat step twice.

Arrange your planter and place it on the hanger that you have made.

Nail to the wall and enjoy seeing your mini planter!

Project 23: Amazing Macramé Curtain

Macramé Curtains give your house the feel of that beach house look. You do not even have to add any trinkets or shells—but you can if you want to. Anyway, here is a great Macramé Curtain that you can make!

Supplies:

- Laundry rope (or any kind of rope/cord you want)
- Curtain rod
- Pins
- Lighter
- Tape

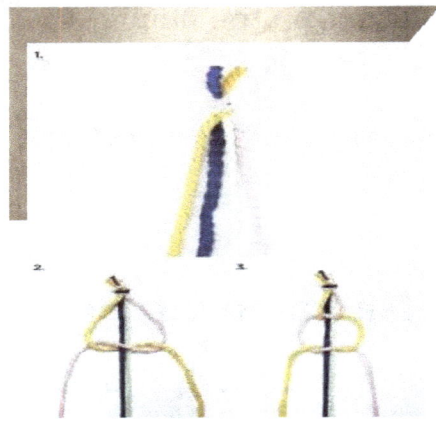

Tie four strands together and secure the top knots with pins so they could hold the structure down.

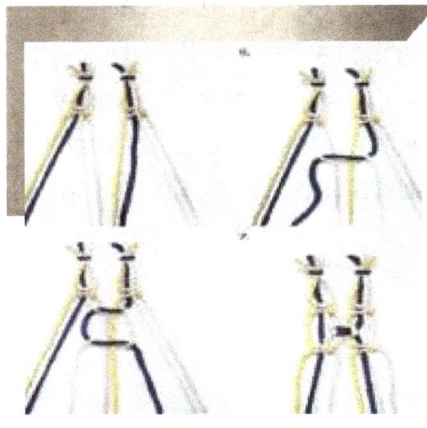

Take the strand on the outer right part and let it cross over to the left side by means of passing it through the middle. Tightly pull the strings together and reverse what you have done earlier.

Repeat crossing the thread over four more times for

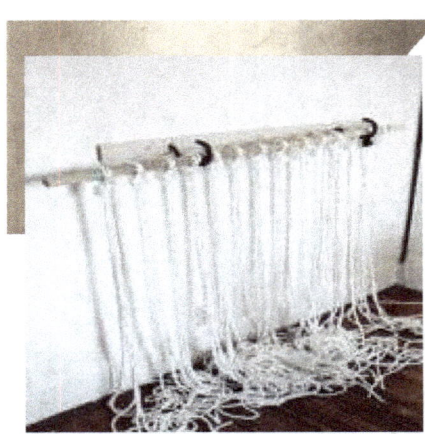

the thread you now have in front of you. Take the strand on the outer left and let it pass through the middle, and then take the right and let it cross over the left side. Repeat as needed, then divide the group of strands to the left,

MACRAMÉ PROJECTS

and to the right. Repeat until you reach the number of rows you want.

You can now apply this to the ropes. Gather the number or ropes you want—10 to 14 is okay, or whatever fits the rod, with good spacing. Start knotting at the

top of the curtain until you reach your desired length. You can burn or tape the ends to prevent them from unraveling.

Braid the ropes together to give them that dreamy, beachside effect, just like what you see below.

That's is, it, you can now use your new curtain!

Project 24: Macramé Wall Art

Adding a bit of Macramé to your walls is always

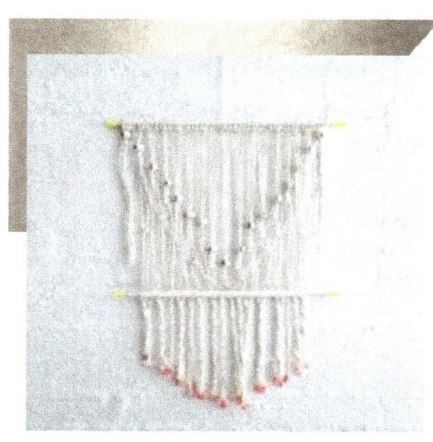

fun because it livens up the space without making it cramped—or too overwhelming for your taste. It also looks beautiful without being too complicated to make. You can check it out below!

Supplies:

- Large wooden beads
- Acrylic paint
- Painter's tape
- Paintbrush
- Wooden dowel
- 70 yards rope

Attach the dowel to a wall. It is best to just use removable hooks, so you will not have to drill anymore.

Cut the rope into 14 x 4 pieces, as well as 2 x 5 pieces. Use 5-yard pieces to end the dowel with. Continue doing this with the rest of the rope.

Then, start making double half-hitch knots and continue all the way through, like what is shown below.

Once you get to the end of the dowel, tie the knots diagonally so that they would not fall or unravel in any way. You can also add the wooden beads any way you want, so you would get the kind of décor that you need. Make sure to tie the knots after doing so.

Use four ropes to make switch knots and keep the décor more secure. Tie around 8 of these.

Add a double half hitch and then tie them diagonally once again.

Add more beads and then trim the ends of the rope.

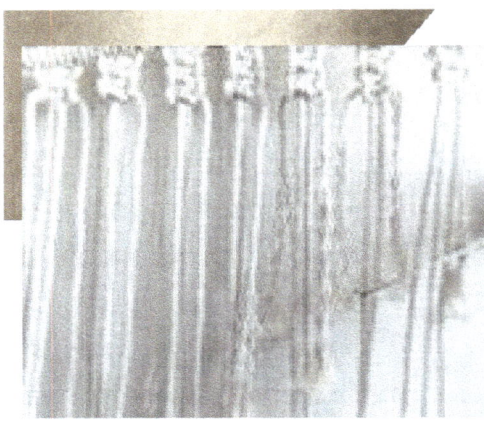

Once you have trimmed the rope, go ahead, and add some paint to it. Summery or neon colors would be good.

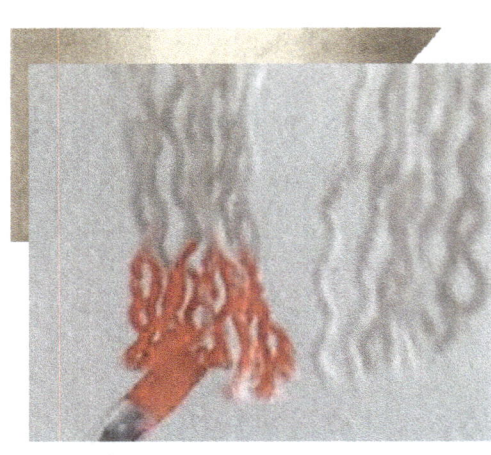

That is, it! You now have your own Macramé Wall Art!

Project 25: Hanging Macramé Vase

To add a dainty, elegant touch to your house, you 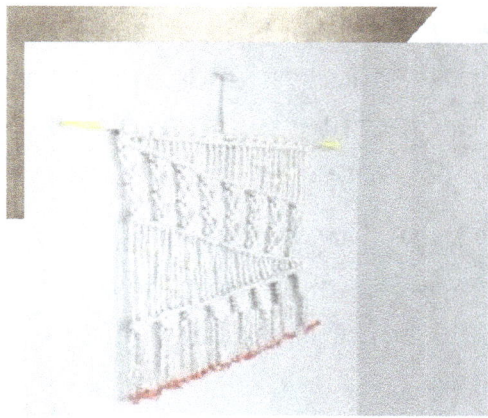 could create a Macramé Vase. With this one, you will have to make use of basket stitches/knots—which You will learn about below. It is also perfect for those who really love flowers—and want to add a touch of nature at home!

Supplies:

- Masking tape
- Tape measure or ruler
- 30 meters thick nylon cord
- Small round vase (with around 20 cm diameter)

 Cut eight cords measuring 3.5 yards or 3.2 meters each and set aside one of them. Cut a cord that measures 31.5 inches and set it aside, as well. Then, cut one cord that measures 55 inches.

Now, group eight lengths of cord together—the ones you did not set aside, of course, and mark the center with a piece of tape.

Wrap the cords by holding them down together and take around 80 cm of it to make a tail—just like what you see below.

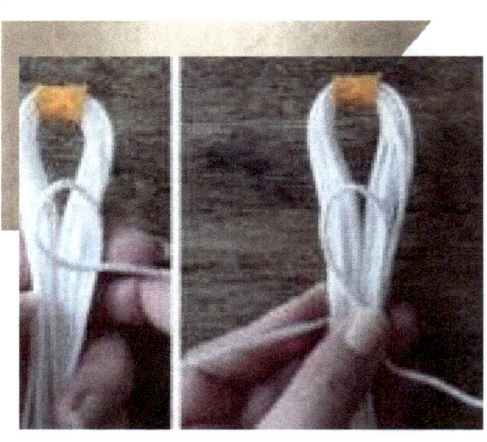

Wrap the cord around the back of the long section and make sure to keep your thumb on the tail. Then, wrap the cord around the main cord group. Make sure it is firm, but do not make it too tight. If you can make the loop bigger, that would be good, too.

Do it 13 more times through the loop and go and pull the tail down so the loop could soften up. Stop letting the cords overlap by pulling them whenever necessary and then cut both ends so they would not be seen anymore.

Divide the cords into groups of four and secure the ends with tape.

Get the group of cords that you have not used yet and make sure to measure 11.5 inches from the beginning—or on top. Do the overhand knot and get the cord on the left-hand side. Fold it over two of the cords and let it go under the cord on the right-hand side.

Fold the fourth cord and let it pass under the leftmost cord then up the loop of the first cord. Make sure to push it under the large knot so that it would be firm.

Make more half-hitches until you form more twists. Stop when you see that you have made around 12 of them and then repeat with the rest of the cords.

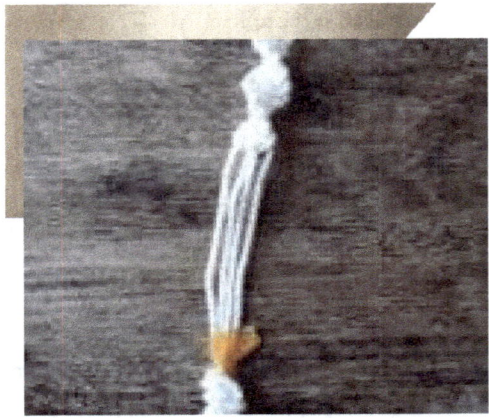

Now, it is time to make the basket for the vase. What you must do here is measure 9 centimeters from your group of cords. Tie an overhand knot and make sure to mark with tape.

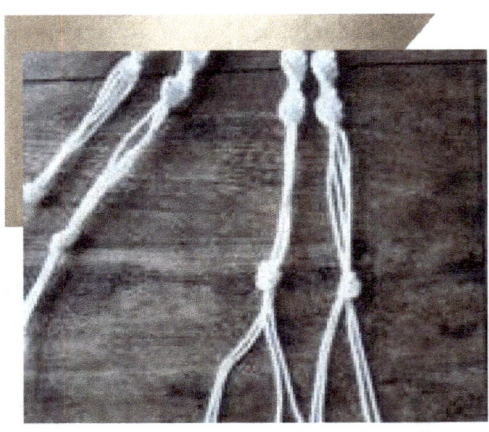

Let the two cord groups come together by laying them side by side.

Tie the cords down but make sure to keep them flat. Make sure that the knots will not overlap, or else you would have a messy project—which is not what you would want to happen. Use two cords from the left as starting point and then bring the two cords on the right over the top of the loop. Loop them together under the bottom cords and then work them back up once more.

Now, find your original loop and thread the same cords behind them. Then, let them pass through the left-hand cords by making use of the loop once more.

Let the knot move once you already have it in position. It should be around 3 inches or 7.5 cm from the overhand knots. After doing so, make sure that you flatten the cords and let them sit next to each other until you have a firm knot on top. Keep dividing and letting cords come together.

Next, get the cord on the left-hand side and let it go over the 2nd and 3rd cords before folding the fourth one under the first two cords. You would then see a square knot forming between the 2nd and 3rd cords. You should then repeat the process on the right-hand side. Open the cord on the right side and let it go under the left-hand cord. Repeat this process thrice, then join the four-square knots that you have made by laying them out on a table.

You will then see that the cords have come together at the base. Now, you must start wrapping the base by wrapping a 1.4-meter cord and wrap around 18 times.

To finish, just cut the cords the way you want. It is okay if they are not of the same length so that there would be variety—and they would look prettier on your wall. Make sure to tie overhand knots at the end of each of them before placing the vase inside.

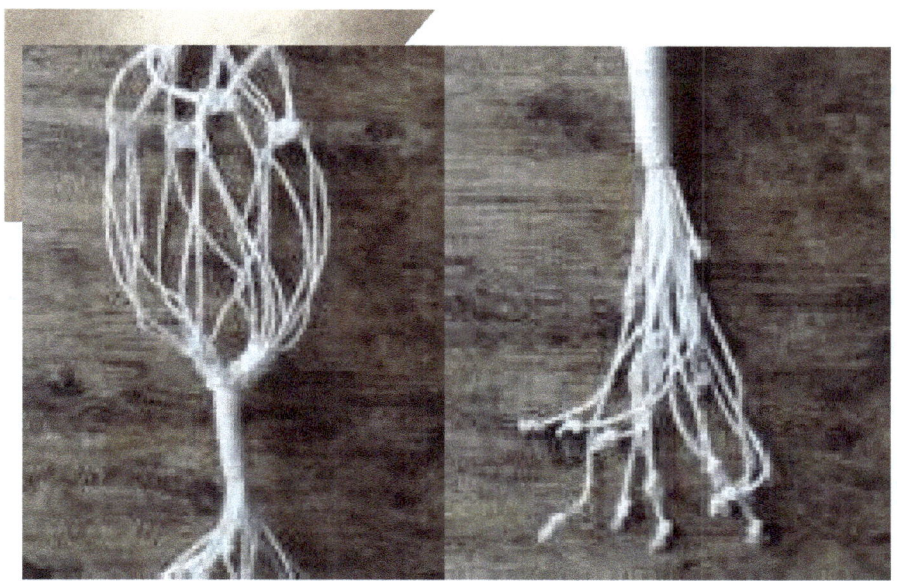

Enjoy your new hanging vase!

CHAPTER - 11
OTHER THINGS YOU CAN DO IN MACRAME

Project 26: Easy DIY Macramé Plant Holder

This is not the macramé of your grandma. All right, maybe it is, but at some point, something makes a comeback or another right? I love this macramé plant holder's smooth and textured feel. And the best part, the best part? It can be done in a few minutes! I am all about basic projects that can be completed in a couple of minutes.

Project 27: Macramé Plant Holder

This is a perfect project to make extra yarn scraps for friends and family. You can use live plants in your bowl, or you can use a fake one if you are a plant killer like me. Any watering? No watering? That is up my alley—let us start now!

Supplies:

- Macramé Plant Holder Materials
- Metal or wooden ring
- Yarn
- Scissors
- Potted plant

Methods

1. Cut four different yarn lengths. Mine were about 2 feet long–you want to make sure that your plant holder is enough to finish! You may need to make the yarn strands even longer, depending on how big your planter is.

2. Fold half the strands of your yarn, then loop the folded end of your chain. Take the loose ends and pull them through the yarn loop you created.

3. Split the yarn into four yarn groupings of two yarn

strands each.

4. Measure several centimeters (I just looked at it) and tie each of the groupings together. Ensure that the knots are about the same length.

5. Document this ad take the left path of each group and add it to the right way of the grouping. Keep the knots a little deeper, from the first set of knots only an inch or two. I know it sounds complicated, but It is not, I swear! Take the two external threads and bind them together to create a circular network.

6. Tie one additional round of knots, repeating the process of knotting each group's left strand to the right strand of the. Bring the ties close to the last round you made–just half or two inches away this time.

7. Tie all the threads of yarn a little under the last round of knots you made around one inch. Cut off the extra yarn to create a beautiful tassel!

Project 28: Easy DIY Macramé Wall Hanging

A macramé wall suspended in a home

A macramé wall hanging is an easy DIY project, which adds a handmade touch to every room in your home. Do not be afraid of turning it into your own.

Given its size, this is a simple project that takes you

an hour or two to finish. It gets together quickly, and you will find many ways of adding your style.

This is only one of many free macramé patterns including plant hangers, curtains and much more.

The knots you use to mount this macramé wall include the head knot, the spiral knot, and the square knot.

What you will need to finish this macramé DIY hanging wall:

Cotton macramé cord (200 feet) and 61 meters (3/4-inch circumference, 24) wooden dwell (3/4, "24-inch) scissors I have been using cotton clothesline on my macramé string. It looks entirely natural and is quite cheap.

The wooden dowel must not be such exact measurements and use whatever scale you like in place of the wood dowel if all ropes are placed over it. If you want to give it an outdoor experience, you can use a branch of a tree about the same height.

Project 29: Make a Hanger for Your Wooden Dowel

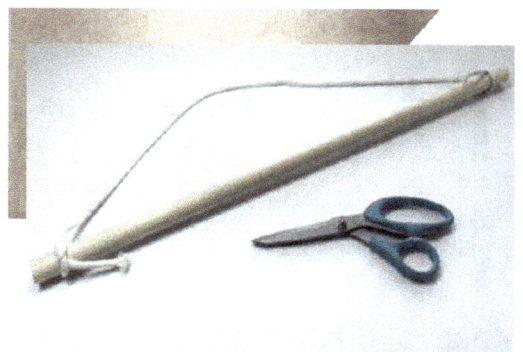

Cut a piece of macramé cord that is three feet (1 meter) and tied to a wooden dowel. Connect the two sides of the wooden dowel to each end of the thread. You are going to use this to mount your macramé project when it is over. In the beginning, I like to attach it, so I can hang up the macramé project when I tie knots. It is much easier to work this way than to determine it.

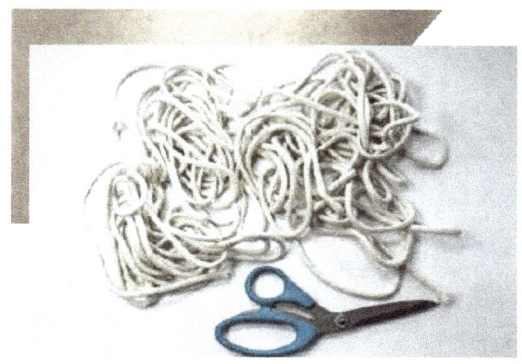

Cut your macramé rope into 12 string lengths 15 feet (4.5 meters) long with the pair of scissors. It might sound like a lot of rope, but knots take up more cord than you expect. If you need it, there is no way to make the rope thicker, so you better cut it than you will.

Fold one of the macramé cores in half on the wooden dowel and use a ladle's head knot to tie it to a wooden dowel

Join the other cords in the same way

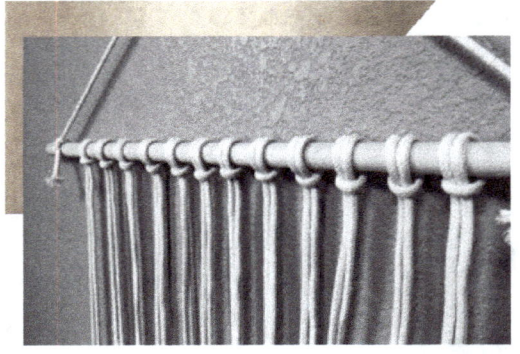

Take the first four strings and make left facing spiral stitch (also referred to as a half-knot Lynton) by tying 13 half knots.

Using four rope to make a further spiral stitch of 13 half knots using the same pair of four ropes. Continue to work in four-chord. You should have a minimum of six spiral stitches before you finish.

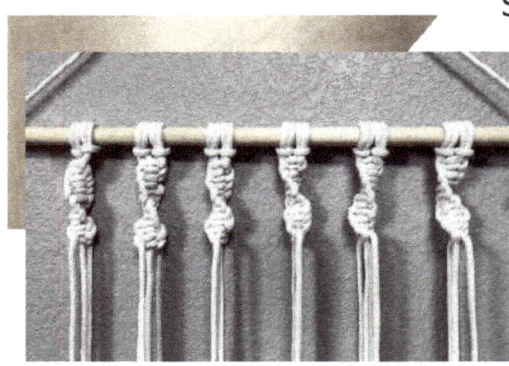

Scale about two inches down from the last knot in a spiral point. This is where your knot, the square knot, will be found.

Make a right knot profile with the first four strings. Continue to make the correct knots face throughout this row. Do your best to keep them all even horizontally. You are going to end up with six knots together.

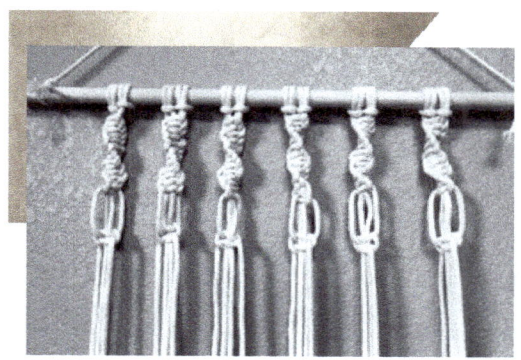

The second row of square knots now is the time to start the square knots so we can have the knots "V" shape

Set open the first two strings and the last two strings. Consider each group of four right-facing square knots. You now have a second line with the first two and last two unknotted cords and five square knots. It does not matter how you space them; just keep them for each row together.

Keep Decreasing the Square knots A "V" formed from the square knots in the third row, the first four strings and the last four strings will be left out. You are going to have four knots together. For the fourth row at the top, leave six cords and at the end six cords. You are going to have 3 square ties. In the fifth row, in the beginning, you will have eight cords and at the end eight cords. Now you are going to have two square ties. For the sixth and final row, ten cords at the beginning and ten cords at the end are to be released. It lets you make a last square knot with four strings.

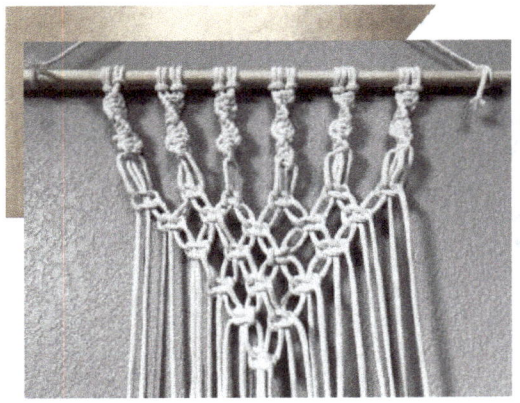

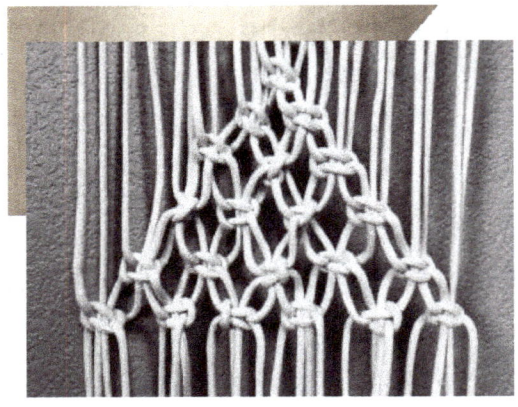

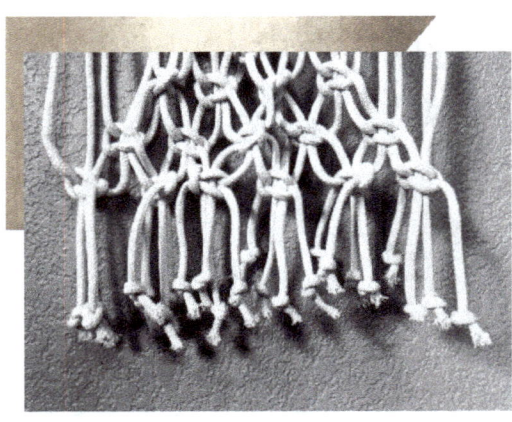

Square Knots Square Making a second "V' in square knots time we will increase them into a triangle or an upside-down" V "For this first segment, bring out the first eight and last eight cords. That will make two square knots.

You already know the term macramé whether you grew up in the 1970s or have been on Pinterest for several years. Macramé models have elaborate designs with a variety of knots which come in different shapes and sizes.

The most common examples on the internet are wall

MACRAMÉ PROJECTS

hangings, but with this technique and material, you can do much more. And while we are still looking forward to one of these exciting projects, we have decided to move the focus away from the wall and to more practical concepts.

Such macramé tutorials are ideal for beginners, and some of them can be completed without a single node. A demonstration lacks nodes at all but uses macramé cord for spinning instead. Would you like to learn more? See below favorite examples.

Nonetheless, first, learn how to make a few simple macramé knots before you launch any of the following projects. Practice these knots until you are confident in the result as much as possible.

A macramé Table Runner

A Beautiful Mess Most macramé table runners are out there, but we love that by A Beautiful Mess. The photos break the pattern into simple steps, and the instructions are straightforward. It can be challenging to figure out how to make a knot without a recording, but these pictures give you a good idea of what every knot will look like.

I talk in layers of co-ordination and contrasts when decorating every room. Such three elements that make a room less simple, regardless of whether it is color, texture, or scale. My fourth guideline is polyvalence! This macramé table runner checked all boxes and made this compact nook with its basic and intriguing style even more unique.

All you need to know is three essential nodes, and you have a charming layer that works every season. If you know the knots learned here, you can tailor your table runner to the length of your table or change it totally and create a hanging macramé wall.

Supply: -12″ wooden dowel −22 lengths of cotton rope measuring 3 mm −with cotton twine − 2″ with dowel hanger scissors

Step One: Apply cotton twine to each end of the dowel and hang it on the door hanger. Fold your first 16″ rope strand in half and create a knot on your dowel. For even more thorough measures, see this article.

Step Two: Keep each 16′ rope strand with a lark's head knot until you have a total of 22. This will allow you to work with 44 strands.

Step 3: Cast the outside right cable across all the other cables (left) and drop the end of your door handle. This will form the basis of the series of knots known as a half-hitch to create a horizontal row. Use the second rope from the right side to tie a knot around the rope you have just draped so that It is 6″ below the dowel.

Step Four: Use the same beach to tie a second knot to the foundation line. This is regarded as a halving knot.

Step Five: Make sure they are clear and even.

Step Six: Repeat from the outside with the second,

MACRAMÉ PROJECTS

third and fourth ropes and tie another hitch-knot, so it is snug, etc. You are going to begin to see the trend. It is a half-hitch horizontal.

Step 7: Continue to tie successive cords throughout a single knot. You do not want to be so close that It is at the edges in the distance.

Step 8: From the right again, use the four outer strands to build a knot about 1.5" below the horizontal knots. See this macramé storage article for more information on a square knot.

Out the four (five to eight) strands then tie another knot of nine to twelve strands. Keep skipping four before you cross the line.

Step Nine: begin again on the right, use the four strands that you skipped (five to eight) and tie a square knot about 3" below the dowel.

Step Ten: Continue tying four-strand sets in square knots until the row is ended.

CONCLUSION

There you have it, well done, everything you need to know to get you started with your own macramé knots. You learned just how easy it is to get started in this hobby, and once you get the hang of things, you are going to find that it is easier than ever to get started with your own projects.

The beauty of Macramé as a vintage art that has survived extinction for centuries and has continued to thrive as a technique of choice for making simple but sophisticated items is simply unrivalled. The simple fact that you have decided to read this manual means that you are well on your way to making something great. There is truly a certain, unequaled feeling of satisfaction that comes from crafting your own masterpiece.

The most important rule in Macramé is the maxim: "Practice makes perfect". If you cease to practice constantly, your skills are likely to deteriorate over time. So, keep your skills sharp, exercise the creative parts of your brain, and keep creating mind-blowing handmade masterpieces. Jewelry and fashion accessories made with even the most basic Macramé knots are always a beauty to behold, hence they serve as perfect gifts for loved ones on special occasions. Presenting a Macramé bracelet to someone, for instance passes the message that you did not just remember to get them a gift, you also treasure them so much that you chose to invest your time into crafting something unique specially for them too, and trust me, that is a very powerful message. However, the most beautiful thing about Macramé is perhaps the fact that it helps to create durable items. Hence you can keep a piece of decoration, or a fashion accessory you made for yourself for many years, enjoy the value and still feel nostalgic anytime you remember when you made it. It even feels better when you made that item with someone. This feature of durability also makes Macramé accessories incredibly perfect gifts.

Macramé can also serve as an avenue for you to begin your dream small business. After perfecting your Macramé skills, you can conveniently sell your items and get paid well for your products, especially if you can perfectly make items like bracelets that people buy a lot. You could even train people and start your own little company that makes bespoke Macramé fashion accessories. The opportunities that Macramé presents are truly endless.

Remember that each of these knots is going to be the foundation of the other projects that you create, so you are going to have to take the time to get familiar with each of them – and practice them until they are what you need them to be. You are not likely going to get them perfectly right away – so take the time to make sure you do it right before you move on to the succeeding one.

Do not worry if you do not get it at first, it is going to come with time, and the more time you put into it, the better you are going to become. It does take time and effort to get it right, but the more time and effort you put into it, the better you are going to be. My goal with this is to give you the inspiration and direction you need to master macramé.

It can be difficult at first, but the more you put into it, the easier It is all going to become until it is just second nature to you. I know you are going to fall in love with each and every aspect of this hobby, and when you know how to work the knots, you are going to want to make them in all the ways you possibly can.

Do not worry about the colors, and do not worry if you do not get it right the first time. This is going to give you everything you need to make it happen the way you want it to, and it is going to show you that you really can have it all with your macramé projects.

I hope you become a master at this hobby, and that you can get the projects you want from the patterns you use. There is no end to the ways you can create macramé projects, and the more familiar you become with them, the easier it is going to be for you to make them no matter what you want them to be. So, dive into the world of macramé with both feet, and learn that there is nothing that is going to stand in your way when it comes to these projects.

So, what are you waiting for? All It is going to take is your time and effort, and you are going to get just what you are after with your macramé projects. From now on, you are on the path to be a macramé master, and you are going to fall in love with everything macramé. The world of macramé awaits, just begging you to dive in and get started.

Good luck and create to your heart's content.

So, stay sharp, keep practicing and keep getting better. Welcome to a world of infinite possibilities!

Stop reading, start doing!